Buying & Selling Property in Florida
A UK Residents Guide

Copyright © 2006 Stephen Parnell
All rights reserved.
ISBN: 1-4196-3290-6
Library of Congress Control Number: 2006902618

To order additional copies, please contact us.
BookSurge, LLC
www.booksurge.com
1-866-308-6235
orders@booksurge.com

STEPHEN
PARNELL

BUYING & SELLING PROPERTY IN FLORIDA A UK RESIDENTS GUIDE

2006

Buying & Selling Property in Florida
A UK Residents Guide

CONTENTS

Introduction xiii
Getting There 1
Holidays and Short Visits 1
Longer Stays/Split Residence 1
Working In Florida 1
Starting Your Own Business 2
Citizenship 2
Buying A Home In Florida 5
Introduction 5
Why Are You Buying A Property In Florida? 5
Where To Buy 7
Regions Of Florida 8
Orlando 8
The Florida Coastline 8
Gold Coast 8
The Panhandle 9
When Local Really Does Mean Local 9
Location, Location, Location 10
Coastal Considerations 11
What Goes Around 13
Broad Similarities 14
Local Differences 15
Jumping On The Roundabout 17
Prices Go Up 17
Prices Go Down 17
Ride The RollerCoaster 18
Just Answer The Question! 19
Finding The Right Property 21
For sale board 21

Agent's property magazine or newspaper 22
For Sale by Owner board 22
Direct from the developer 22
Newspaper/Magazine adverts in the UK 23
From a guide book 24
At an exhibition or seminar. 24
Foreclosure/REO Properties. 25
Do it yourself 25
With the help of a buyer's agent 26
Buyer's Agents 27
Follow The Money 27
Legal Responsibilities 28
The Right Agent For You 28
Closing The Deal 31
The Deal Isn't Closed Until. 31
Time Is Of The Essence. 32
Trusted Advisors. 33
Mortgage Agent 33
Independent Appraiser 33
Home Inspector 35
...And More Reports. 36
Pest Inspection 36
Bad News? 36
Home Warranties 37
Finally. 39
Financing Property In Florida 41
Introduction 41
Mortgage Types 43
Fixed Rate Mortgages 43
Adjustable Rate Mortgages 43
Interest Only Loans. 44
"Equity Builder" Mortgage 44
Special Case Mortgages 44
The Option ARM 44

Mortgages For Rental Properties 46
Mortgage Miscellanea. 49
Mortgage Availability 49
Mortgage Affordability 49
Pre-Approved Mortgages. 49
Dollar or Sterling Mortgage? 51
All The Fees 51
Taxing Concerns. 55
Resident Or Not? 56
Tax On Income 56
Sales Tax. 56
Insurance 59
Homeowners Insurance 59
How To Save Money on Homeowners Insurance. 60
Title Insurance 62
Flood Insurance. 63
Money Matters 65
US Bank Accounts 65
Currency Conversion 65
Escrow Accounts. 67
Managing A Home In Florida 69
Introduction 69
The Economics Of Rental 71
The Economics Of Property Rental 71
Guaranteed Rental Income 71
Slim Margins 72
Management Companies 73
Before You Start 73
Rental Options 73
Who Does What?. 74
Choosing A Management Company. 75
Property Management Services .76
Propert Management Costs 77
The Business Of Property Rental 79
Dealing With The State 79

Insurance Matters	80
Selling A Home In Florida	81
Introduction	81
Why Are You Selling?	81
Timing	83
For Sale By Owner	85
Seller's Agents	89
Time To Promote	91
Setting The Price	91
Sell, Sell, Sell	93
Check The Price	93
Check The Condition	93
Location, location, location	94
Promotion	94
Market Problems	95
Open All Hours	95
Easy Improvements	95
Tax For Sellers	97
Capital Gains	97
Foreign Investors Real Property Tax Act	97
Inheritance tax	98
Appendix A: Glossary	99

INTRODUCTION

Florida holds a special place in the hearts and minds of many British people.

The availability of affordable transatlantic flights, combined with the draw of major tourist attractions has created a massive holiday industry specifically tailored to Brits holidaying in Florida. With many of these holidaymakers living in rented accommodation rather than hotels during their stay in the "Sunshine State" it's not surprising that many of them get a real taste for the Florida lifestyle and look for a way to make it a bigger part of their lives.

Some go as far as to make a permanent move, taking up employment or starting their own business in Florida. Others postpone their move until retirement provides the opportunity for a major lifestyle change and a permanent move to Florida.

The largest group however satisfy their desires by the purchase of property in Florida to provide a personal holiday base, subsidised by renting out the property to other holidaymakers. Done properly, this can give you a fantastic holiday home, a good steady return on your investment, and an appreciating asset. Hardly surprising it's an attractive proposition for thousands of families every year.

The incredible level of demand has spawned an entire industry that makes its living selling Florida property—and associated service—to the Brits. Unfortunately, the quality of advice and information given to these buyers isn't always what it might be, and it is all too common for the outcome to be unsatisfactory when buying property in Florida.

It seems that many people think that because there are so many similarities between our countries and the language we speak; it is safe to assume that the systems for buying property, the appropriate laws and customs that apply—will all be the same too.

Of course, this is far from true and there are many potential pitfalls for the unsuspecting British buyer. However, these can all be safely negotiated with a little advance research and by selecting the right advisors to help you in your quest.

Reading this book is an excellent start!

Never, ever make the mistake of assuming something will work a certain way because that is what would happen in the UK—and never assume that anyone will highlight the differences for you…

…Unless of course you have sensibly enlisted the help of someone who is specifically experienced in the exact business of helping British people buy property in Florida. That is really the only guaranteed way of getting through the process from start to finish without tears. It isn't enough to work only with people who understand the Florida system—if they don't also have some understanding of the system *you* are familiar with they will not know what they have to focus on to help you with the critical differences between the two.

Since I moved from the UK to Florida in 1991, I've built up a massive amount of experience in helping UK citizens successfully buy, finance, manage and sell properties here.

This book is a distillation of that experience and I think it's unique in its field—because it is a truly independent guide based on personal knowledge, not simply a vehicle for advertising developments and services like most of the so-called "guides" to Florida property.

Buying property in Florida is a high-stakes game. The lifestyle, income and security that come from a well-researched and properly executed plan are immensely positive and can change your life—but the price you pay for mistakes can of course be equally significant.

Fortunately, I know how to do this properly and how to avoid the pitfalls along the way, so I look forward to helping you achieve your dream of becoming the owner of property in Florida!

GETTING THERE

There always seems to be a lot of confusion around things like visas and green cards—and in these times of increased security-consciousness it may be that the situation will seem to get even more confusing.

Much of this lack of clarity is due to the wide variety of different visas that exist for different purposes. In practice there are only a few that cater for the vast majority of people buying property in Florida.

Holidays and Short Visits

Most people can simply visit the USA for up to 90 days at a time without a visa under the "Visa Waiver Program". This is ideal for research visits when considering your plans and will cover most holiday trips to enjoy your own property.

Longer Stays/Split Residence

A "B-2" visa is still a tourist visa, but it allows you to stay in the USA for up to six months at a time. This would be suitable for example for a retired person who wants to spend half of each year in the UK and half in Florida. You can actually spend more of each year in Florida if you break up your visits, but you have to be careful not to abuse the system (by leaving the USA for a week and then returning for example) or the visa will be revoked.

Working In Florida

If you are moving to Florida because of employment, there are various visa programs to allow this, but they are aimed at executives, skilled and professional workers. All assume the employment is current and they are not designed to allow people to enter the USA looking for work.

The requirements for these "L" and, "H" visas vary, but your employer will probably have gone through the process with other workers and will know how it worked.

Starting Your Own Business

Getting a visa that will allow you to do business in Florida on a long-term basis is a good deal more complicated. Although there are well-established mechanisms and high success rates (assuming you meet the criteria) to facilitate this process, it is by no means guaranteed that you will be successful. The most common—indeed, typically the only—visa for people setting up in business, is the E-2 "investor" visa.

This is one of the more complex types of entry visa, and there is extensive documentation to be completed. You may consider recruiting the assistance of a specialist who can guide you not only through the application process, but can advise you in detail as to what features of the businesses you consider will affect your chances of visa success.

In short, you will have to prove that you have committed significant funds to the creation of a US business that can support you, your dependents and will create employment for local people.

Citizenship

All visas have to be renewed periodically, so you may eventually decide to make Florida your permanent home and try for the fabled "Green Card".

The first thing to be clear about is that American citizenship is quite separate from your visa status, and having any previous visas is completely unrelated to your chances of ever becoming a citizen. There are essentially six ways you might get a Green Card:

- **Multinational Manager.** If you reach a point where you have substantial businesses in both the UK and the USA, the Multinational Manager program may be the easiest way to get a Green Card.

- **Relative Sponsorship.** A close relative who is a US citizen can sponsor you. This might be a path for example if a child becomes a US citizen through marriage, as they can then sponsor you.
- **Employer Sponsorship.** For example, a child or spouse may become a citizen through the sponsorship of their employer——and then in turn sponsor their parent or partner.
- **Investment.** If you invest $1,000,000 (less in some areas) in a business that creates at least 10 new jobs——that alone can qualify you for a Green Card.
- **PPEA.** Professionals and People of Extraordinary Ability. This program grants immediate residency to key professionals in high demand sectors (notably health care) and to athletes, artists, researches and so on who can prove extraordinary ability n their chosen field.
- **Lottery.** There is an annual lottery that allocates residency to a small number of people in different countries.

With the exception of basic tourist visas, it is probably worth recruiting the services of an immigration lawyer or similar service, as there are many criteria that are firmly believed or definitely known to be in place, but are not documented anywhere for the layman.

DIY applications are very likely to fail after long delays and may count against future applications.

BUYING A HOME IN FLORIDA

INTRODUCTION

Why Are You Buying A Property In Florida?
That might seem like a stupid question—but the exact answer can influence many aspects of the information that follows in this book.

If you are making a permanent move to Florida and are buying a home to live in all year round for the rest of your life, that is a very different proposition from buying a property that you hope to finance through rental income. Buying a property with a view to trading up in a few years is different from choosing a property to enjoy for your whole retirement.

Your choice of location, style of house, the type of finance you choose—indeed, the type of finance available to you—are all likely to be different depending on exactly what your plans and aspirations are.

So, I strongly recommend that you sit down with your partner, your family and any other interested parties and think through your answer to that question before you go much further. Discuss considerations like "How far into the future are we planning?" and what you would do if the unexpected happened—for example, how would things like serious ill health in the family or redundancy affect your plans or your attitude towards your property in Florida?

WHERE TO BUY

Florida sits at the southern tip of the United States of America. The "panhandle" extends along the northern edge of the Gulf of Mexico, and the larger peninsula extends southwards between the Atlantic Ocean to the east and the Gulf of Mexico to the west.

Florida describes itself as the "world's entertainment capital and leading holiday destination", a status that owes as much to the efforts of the state legislature as it does to the legendary climate.

The popularity of the state as a destination has also created a massive industry catering specifically for property purchases by overseas residents—especially from the UK.

However, it is all too easy for British buyers to be blinded by the photographs and videos showing beautiful new American-style houses and nicely landscaped plots all in a pristine setting in the "Sunshine State". They forget what the golden rule of property buying—location, location, location—really means.

Sitting in the dismal UK winter, they think the "location" is Florida, and that everything—anything—in Florida is an attractive alternative.

They forget that Florida is a massive state, and there are the same regional variations within the state as there are in the UK. The decision to buy a property in Miami or Orlando, on the Gulf coast, the Atlantic coast, or in central Florida can be critically important—especially if some or all of the mortgage is to be paid by holiday rentals. You wouldn't think that buying a property in Liverpool was interchangeable with buying in the Lake District, so don't make the same mistake with Florida.

Regions Of Florida

Orlando

Orlando is a world-class, large-scale tourist destination, with some 60 million visitors each year. With a massive range of established and new tourist attractions, reasonable proximity to the coast and easy air links to the UK, this is the largest single area for property investment in Florida.

At first, life in Orlando may seem very exciting—frenetic even—based around theme parks (Orlando is home to Disney World, Universal and MGM Studios, Pleasure Island, Sea World and many, many more), shopping and eating out. However, the scale of the area, careful zoning and surrounding countryside mean Orlando can also be a location that is peaceful, private and relaxing.

Although Orlando and nearby Kissimmee are about as far inland as anywhere in Florida, the coast is still only about 45 minutes away. Being inland does mean that properties here are not subjected to the same weather extremes as those on the coast—which could mean a saving on insurance if nothing else!

The Florida Coastline

Over 1000 miles of glorious sandy beaches, palm trees and warm clear blue water, combined with a great year-round climate means the Florida coast can be a good choice to maximise rental income.

Extending over such a large area means "the coast" takes in a wide variety of different locations, each with their own local flavours.

Gold Coast

A narrow coastal strip with golden beaches bordering the Atlantic Ocean and the Everglades, is where you will find many popular locations such as Fort Lauderdale, Boca Raton, Miami and

Palm Beach. Life on the entire Atlantic coast is considered to be a little more hectic than on the relaxed Gulf coast.

Space Coast

The area in the centre of the Atlantic coast is where you will find famous names such as the Kennedy Space Centre, Cape Canaveral and Daytona Beach.

Gulf Coast

The west Coast of Florida is an area of exceptional beauty, featuring a shoreline of coral inlets with white sandy beaches. Outdoor living is the norm here, whether your tastes extend to golf and tennis, or the more adventurous scuba diving and water skiing. Equally, properties in this area are very varied—from waterfront homes to condominiums in beach and golf course developments.

This is an area where life tends to go at a more relaxed pace and areas such as Sarasota, Fort Myers and Naples are becoming more and more popular with US and UK citizens looking for the climate and lifestyle benefits of Florida without the brashness of Orlando and Miami Beach.

The Panhandle

The northern region of Florida borders the states of Alabama and Georgia, so cities such as Pensacola have a character closer to "the deep south" than to the glitzy glamour of Miami for example.

You can get a "visitor's-eye view" of Florida at VisitFlorida.com, the official tourist website for the state. This will give you a destination-by-destination view of the kind of official promotion that goes into bringing visitors to Florida, and how the state is branding the different areas and promoting them to different target groups.

When Local Really Does Mean Local

Even when you have narrowed down your search to a region, and then further to a specific city or area, you have to be aware of an important location factor that will influence your choice of property—local zoning.

In many areas, local zoning is similar to the broad classification of land in the UK—specifying what it can be used for; residential, agricultural, industrial etc. However, there are local zoning restrictions in Florida that go into much more detail, specifically in relation to residential properties. These can influence all kinds of things, from the number, size and style of houses in the area—to what you can do with them.

The most significant zoning restriction is that only certain areas allow short-term letting, so you can't buy a property as a primary or secondary home (that is—where only you will live in it) and assume you can later decide to start renting it out, as there may be zoning restrictions that prevent this.

Some zoning restrictions even apply to things like the number, size and shape of swimming pools in an area, so you really do need to dig right into the detail before committing to a Florida property.

Some areas have very few properties zoned for short term letting, which may tempt you to dismiss them as a potential place to buy. However, if the area is attractive and the location is right, it's likely that those few properties can enjoy high rental rates and occupancy levels.

Location, Location, Location

Narrowing down your area of interest to a region according to the general lifestyle you want to live—or that you want to offer to your paying guests—is a good start, and it will certainly make the rest of the task more manageable. Making sure your area of interest is zoned for the kind of use you intend means another important hurdle has been jumped.

However, the true meaning of "location, location, location" only comes into play when you look at the next level of detail—the location of specific properties.

It's critical when you are evaluating each potential property that you are able to take some time to blank out completely the building itself, and consider where the building is located—don't fall in love with a building, a swimming pool, or style of décor and allow that to blind you to where it is situated.

Remember—you can change *anything* about a property except its location!

Warning signs that signal "bad" location:
- On a feeder street
- On a flight path
- In or near a gang territory
- Too close to night life
- In a rundown block or area
- Next to a school or school playground
- Next to apartments or commercial property
- In close proximity to a freeway, expressway or railroad
- Next to a petrol station
- Near any disposal or waste facilities
- In an area of high unemployment
- Within reach of odours from factories or farms

Coastal Considerations

Properties on the coast are of course more exposed to the elements than those inland—with implications you must consider when thinking about buying property there.

The most serious implication of course, arises from the fact that Florida is the most hurricane-prone state in the USA. In practical terms, this translates into two risks for homeowners along the coast—wind and flood (the tidal storm surge from a hurricane is termed flooding for insurance purposes).

Along with the asking price of a coastal property, you should also consider the availability and cost of insurance against these risks. It is quite possible that the cost of insuring a coastal property will be twice as high as a property inland, adding a four-figure sum every year to your costs

It is certainly advisable to make any agreement of sale contingent upon getting adequate and affordable insurance.

Wind insurance is generally required if the property is in a 25 mile wide coastal strip, whereas flood insurance is based on official flood zone maps—but many large national companies have stopped offering insurance in Florida because of these requirements. That restricts your ability to shop around, and increases prices.

On the Atlantic coast, the wind insurance is likely to cost much more than flood insurance, while on the Gulf coast the situation will be reversed—but in total the additional cost will be significant on both sides of the peninsula.

I'm certainly not saying that it's a bad idea to buy on the coast—obviously millions of Floridians are doing it quite happily and enjoying the lifestyle—just to make sure you factor in the extra elements to your calculations.

WHAT GOES AROUND

One of the major challenges in choosing a region to buy property in—with a view to rental income, future resale value and saleability—is to understand the various cycles that influence property values. Not only the value of the property today, but also the future value.

Future resale value will be of more concern to some buyers than others. If you are purchasing a property that you plan to live in for the rest of your life—say as a retirement home—then future price trends will be of less interest than if you are looking at the economics of a five or 10 year investment period.

Property owners in the UK have now experienced a fairly consistent period of growing property prices over quite a long time. Sometimes the growth has been moderate, sometimes—and in some parts of the country in particular—it has been very fast indeed. A large portion of the increased spending power of many families is funded by the rising value of property over the years since the previous generation climbed the first steps of the property ladder.

Consequently, the current generation of British homeowners could be forgiven for assuming that property prices simply keep on rising; it's just what they do. And it's no surprise that when they look at property further afield, British buyers often assume that the same unwritten laws apply in other countries too.

However, such assumptions can be dangerous when considering buying property in Florida. There are enough underlying similarities to make the careless buyer think they are just getting a great deal on amazing properties—but also enough differences to recommend that the careful buyer does their research and enters in to any purchase with their eyes fully open.

Working out how current values and recent trends will influence future values is not easy—yet it's important to have some understanding of these factors when assessing areas you might want to look at in more detail.

Broad Similarities

In the big picture, the USA generally is enjoying a construction boom, driven by the demand of a growing population—especially of the "baby boomer" generation who tend to leave the family home earlier than in the past and more frequently set up home as singles, couples or small families. Add in higher than average salaries and you have all the fuel necessary to drive property prices upwards.

The Florida property market in particular has recently gone through a period of rapid price increases driven by demand in key areas. As in the UK, the developers have responded to the demand by building new homes in record numbers—and the signs are now pointing to an overall slow-down in both supply and demand, with fewer plans in place for new developments, and a flattening of the price increase graph.

Mortgage rates also have an ongoing effect on demand, and predictions for the immediate future are for steady growth in property values—but at a substantially lower rate than in recent years.

Not everyone thinks this is a bad thing. For property owners looking at the long term, an ongoing steady increase in the value of their property is often preferable to the boom and bust cycles that can leave them very uncertain as to their financial security. And for new buyers, slow steady growth means they can take the time necessary to make a considered decision about buying property in Florida without the added pressure of rapidly-increasing prices all around them.

The value of property in the USA is in general tied to the local job market—just like the UK, where the economic draw of the South East has led to recent dramatic price increases. Across the whole of the USA, the last overall drop in property values came in the Depression, when unemployment was as high as 25%. Since then, the general trend has been for more jobs with higher average incomes, resulting in a long period of sustained increase in property values.

Of course, the devil is in the detail, and—just as in the UK—not all areas of the country have enjoyed the same increases. Indeed, even within Florida itself, there are important regional differences that you need to be aware of when considering a property purchase there.

Local Differences

Some of the factors under consideration may seem at first to be very general—almost global in their influence. For example, an adjustment of the value of the dollar against the pound, or an increase in the cost of aviation fuel will affect much more than the price of property in Florida. However, when you consider the significance of Florida as a destination for British holidaymakers, who all arrive by air—the impact of these changes is magnified disproportionately on the Florida property market.

While no-one is predicting a dramatic drop in property prices, the combination of these general factors with specific local situations suggest that potential buyers should keep a watchful eye on values across the state.

Orlando, for example, has for the longest time been almost synonymous with Florida in the minds of British tourists, many of whom looked no further a field when deciding to buy property. This has resulted in a dramatic rise in the number of British-owned short-term let properties. A large proportion of these were bought during a period of booming prices, funded by mortgages that were calculated on attractive exchange rates and optimistic occupation levels.

It is possible that in the near future, these owners will have to lower their expectations, especially if factors such as the aforementioned exchange rates and travel costs result in significantly reduced visitor numbers (and rental incomes). Under these circumstances, many of these owners may choose to bail out of the market, creating a glut of rental-level properties and no doubt impacting on values.

It is also fair to say that there have been large numbers of rental properties purchased in popular areas across Florida without enough thought given to the effect of the increasing competition. This has created a large pool of attractive properties—some of which again may become available at lower than expected prices if their rental income cannot cover the owners' costs.

JUMPING ON THE ROUNDABOUT

As you can see, the movement of property values tends to be cyclic in nature. Understanding the various factors that influence the rise and fall of prices will help you choose the right time to buy into a specific area, and when it might be better to pass on what looks like a good deal.

Prices Go Up

Popularity of a certain area leads to an increase in demand and an increase in prices. Rising prices mean owners enjoy high returns on their investment, which in turn makes the area even more attractive to new buyers, driving demand and prices even higher. Land owners, builders and everyone else associated with the process are in high demand, so their prices increase too. More builders move into an area, more land changes hands, more new properties are built. Values rise and rise.

Until…

Something happens to slow down, stop and even reverse the trend.

Prices Go Down

Most often it's simply that the market becomes saturated. There are no longer enough new customers for all the new properties being built, so prices fall.

As prices fall, the value of existing properties falls too. Owners with a strong investment motivation see the value of their assets falling, and sell up—driving prices down further.

Saturation also means more competition for visitors and rentals and a tendency for rental rates to be reduced to attract customers. It also means there are simply not enough visitors to fill all the properties to break-even levels. Losing just a couple of bookings a year can put some owners below their break-even point, so they are forced to sell up as they can't cover the mortgage. More people selling means prices continue to move downwards.

Until...

Again, something happens to slow down, stop and even reverse the trend.

A major new visitor attraction or a landmark development might inject new interest into an area, stimulating new interest in properties within easy travelling distance.

A certain price level may make it of particular interest to a certain type of customer, creating demand for a particular type of property that can ripple outwards to affect the whole area.

Or it might simply become more fashionable due to some change in lifestyle choices, a media event, or high profile residents.

These cycles may happen slowly over many years and there are never any guarantees that the cycle will rise as far as it falls, or even that it will complete the cycle within a typical lifetime.

Ride The RollerCoaster

That might all sound very scary, like I'm warning that your investment is bound to ride a rollercoaster over the coming years, causing you alternating heart attacks and bouts of elation, but it's unlikely to be as dramatic as that.

Rather, what I want to encourage you to do is be wise and keep your eyes open and your brain switched on at all times. As you evaluate an area and the properties within it, you should be assessing not only what is happening in the area today, but also how that might pan out over the next few years.

For example, an area with many new developments is a good sign that an area is "hot"——but you have to be sure you haven't arrived too late in the cycle and buy one of the last full-price properties before the developer starts handing out discounts, incentives and guaranteed income packages to make his sales. A developer offering agents 10% commission on sales can have a dramatic impact on the local marketplace and create a false impression of just what the local property market is like.

Your agent can help you understand things like this as they will have an idea how many properties were being sold on this kind of development last month, three months ago, six months ago—how prices are trending locally, and how quickly properties are selling when they come on the market.

It's also worth remembering that any of these trends can be bucked by buying wisely and financing carefully. Leverage all of the advice and resources available to you to make wise choices rather than simply following the herd and it is certainly possible to find, finance and operate a property that will be substantially trend-proof.

Just Answer The Question!

Ok, in spite of all this talk of cycles, ups and downs, caveats and warnings, everyone looking at buying property in Florida wants to know the same thing. They have seen the way prices have increased over recent years and they want to know "Will Florida property prices just keep on going up and up?"

There's no question that there is a good deal of investor "flipping" in Florida—where someone buys a property (or more commonly puts a deposit on an as-yet uncompleted property) and then sells soon after to realise a profit without ever living in the property. In some cases, a property can be "flipped" several times before it is even fully built.

That's the kind of thing that creates headlines about the big money that can be made in Florida property, and no doubt this will continue to happen for as long as the Florida market maintains it's upwards trajectory. It is not however a plan I would recommend to the man or woman in the street who are gambling with their nest egg.

Firstly, it has to be said that experts agree you should not base any property purchase on the expectation of capital appreciation and therefore the correct answer to the original question would be something like "Don't base your calculations on that assumption."

However, the same kind of experts also say that if you look at the past trends and make an informed forecast into the future, it seems realistic to expect that prices over the next 10 years will rise at a similar rate to the increases over the last 10 years—around nine to 10% per annum.

I say—be very, very aware that those are averages. I'm looking right now at a report for 2005 that showed the *average* statewide increase in median price was 29%. However, that average hides a wide range of local stories, with the lowest *average* increases reported in Tallahassee (10%) and Gainesville (11%) and the highest *average* increases were reported in Melbourne/Titusville/Palm Bay area (36%) and Fort Myers/Cape Coral (44%).

Those seem like great numbers—even at the low end, but remember that those *averages* will conceal some cases where prices fell and people lost money, so you really cannot relax at all and *assume* there will be capital growth in the property you buy—simply treat it as a great bonus when and if it happens.

FINDING THE RIGHT PROPERTY

So, what's the next step in actually finding the right property for you?

You *can* find properties in a number of different ways:
- For Sale board
- Agent's property magazine or newspaper
- For Sale by Owner board
- Direct from the developer
- Newspaper/Magazine adverts in the UK
- From a guide book
- At an exhibition or seminar
- Foreclosure/REO
- Do it yourself
- With the help of a buyer's agent

There's only one of these I can really recommend (can you guess which one?)—but let's take a look at them all briefly for now and then return to them later as required. Forewarned is forearmed as they say!

For sale board

This is a common way to find properties in the UK, but not the best way in Florida. Contacting the vendor or their agent via the details on a sales board potentially ties you into a one-sided deal where all the cards are stacked in favour of the seller. The agent in the middle of such a deal has loyalty *only* to the seller, leaving you very exposed to risk.

In a situation like this, the seller's agent potentially stands to earn double their normal commission (I'll explain why later)—a strong incentive to push through the sale even if they know it's not right for you.

Agent's property magazine or newspaper

This is exactly the same as the item above—I do not advise you to contact sales agents directly yourself.

For Sale by Owner board

Unless for some particular reason you already know the property in question very, very well, this is not a good way to go. Real estate professionals in Florida are heavily regulated, trained and licensed, and have clear responsibilities with regard to fair representation, disclosure etc—all of which you forego if you decide to do a deal direct with the owner.

Direct from the developer

The key thing to remember here is that everyone involved in selling properties on a development site has only one loyalty—to the developer. They receive strong financial incentives to sell not only properties, but also expensive extras—and may even get paid extra for selling the least attractive plots. This is not a buyer-friendly environment!

Buying "off-plan" in a development that is designed specifically for short-term rentals is not in itself necessarily a bad idea—if you do your homework and everything about the deal stacks up.

However, watch out for developments that have been designed and built specifically with this kind of "sell to the Brits" sales model in mind. These properties can be dressed up to look like an attractive proposition to a naïve foreign buyer, but they may (for example) be a very poor candidate for resale—to better-educated foreign buyers or to local families.

You may be quite happy about the idea of spending a few weeks a year in a purpose-built development with no local shops or schools, but you have to think about how that will affect the future resale value. Local families are unlikely to find such developments attractive—not only do they have few amenities, but Florida families do not enjoy living in the middle of rental properties with a constant flow of holidaymakers moving in and out.

...this of course is the reasoning behind the local zoning restrictions that are designed to separate permanent residences from rental properties.

Yes, if you decide to sell, the property may be attractive to other British buyers like you, but bear in mind that the same development company may have built three new developments in the same area by the time you are trying to sell—and are throwing vast marketing budgets behind their efforts to attract buyers to their new developments.

Show Homes

Something else you need to be aware of when buying "off plan" at a development—is the way show homes are handled in Florida. Don't buy a property on a new development thinking that your home will look like the show house!

We're used to show homes in the UK being furnished and dressed to look their best, but a Florida show home is more like the cars they show in the TV ads—metallic paint, air conditioning, alloy wheels and a whole range of other extras that might add 30% or more to the price.

You need to be extremely astute and well informed—a formal architectural or building qualification would be useful—to be sure that you understand the relationship between what you see on the plan and in the show home...and what you are buying.

Indeed, many specialists go further and advise British clients against visiting any developments on spec. There are too many stories of Brits being friendly and open with the on-site agents only to find later that they have been verbally signed up for services, or even worse, property!

Newspaper/Magazine adverts in the UK

Unfortunately, there is no guarantee that a company's marketing budget is in proportion to their construction, maintenance, contingency or any other budgets. Indeed, all too often it seems that large marketing budgets are allocated to disguise shortcomings in other areas. In short, don't believe everything you read!

From a guide book

Guide books are a great way to find out about the permanent features of an area—tourist attractions, climate, quality of beaches and so on—but they are not a good way to get your finger on the pulse of what is happening in a specific property market this year or even this month. Things change in the market too quickly for printed guide books of property listings to keep track, and they are rarely updated enough to keep up with the latest trends.

At an exhibition or seminar

It may be convenient to look at Florida properties in a local exhibition centre rather than going to all the trouble of flying across the Atlantic and getting involved in the market, but it is very unlikely to get you a good deal.

Yes, it's always a good idea to do as much research as you can, and picking up useful information at exhibitions and seminars will help to make you a better-informed buyer—as long as you do enough research to develop snake-oil radar that will prevent you being misled by the smoother operators.

Selling property at a distance is always a high-risk business, and "Florida swampland" is a cliché in America for property that is sold as highly desirable but turns out to be a mosquito-infested swamp. Although you are unlikely to end up buying swampland at a London property seminar these days (unless that's what you really, really want!), there are modern equivalents that can leave you not getting the best property, mortgage or value for money.

Companies with stands at exhibitions—and even more so those running their own seminars—are virtually always representing a very small number of developments, perhaps only one. Combined with all the additional expenses they have in travelling and marketing overseas, you can imagine the pressure their staff are under to get you signed up and earn them a commission. They certainly don't have your best interests at heart, so why would you believe anything they tell you? ...especially when you consider they are conveniently operating outside the jurisdiction of the Florida laws that are designed to regulate real estate transactions in the state!

Foreclosure/REO Properties

An entire industry has grown up around promoting foreclosed properties as a cheap way to get property in key areas like Florida.

They are however quite a risky proposition, as they are typically offered with little or no information about their status—and they may well be offered complete with sitting defaulting tenants who have to be evicted by the new owner!

The amount of research required to minimise the risk—and the number of auctions that have to be attended before you might successfully obtain a foreclosed property—make this unsuitable for most UK citizens looking for property in Florida.

"REO" (Real Estate Owned) properties are a category that may be slightly more practical. These properties have been repossessed by the bank or mortgage company, who have taken care of any issues such as existing occupants—to make the property ready for a more conventional sale.

These can be bargains, as the lender is clearly motivated to sell—but they will typically require additional time and money to get them back to good condition, so this must be factored into your thinking.

Finally, the process of actually doing a deal for a REO property can be quite drawn out, as you are dealing typically with a bank department rather than direct with the owner and their agent.

If you find a property that fits your purposes and it turns out that it is REO, it may be worth investigating further, but I wouldn't recommend British buyers go out expressly looking for foreclosure or REO bargains.

Do it yourself

With the growth in DIY conveyancing in the UK, it's understandable that some people are tempted to try this when buying in Florida.

However, the differences between the real estate systems of the two countries—especially the number of different professionals involved in Florida and the layers of federal, state, and potentially county and even city regulation, make this a very risky proposition. Especially when you consider that the most valuable advisor you can have to help you through the process won't cost you a penny.

With the help of a buyer's agent

The concept of the "buyer's agent" is perhaps the most significant difference in the Florida real estate system that British buyers have to understand. It's so important to the success of your property plans that I'm going to give it a chapter all to itself.

BUYER'S AGENTS

The first thing to understand here is that in Florida, you do not have to trudge around dozens of estate agents to see what properties each of them has on offer.

Virtually every property that is for sale in Florida is listed on a central database system—the Multiple Listing System or MLS—that is available to all Real Estate Agents (Realtors). The MLS can be searched by location, price and other factors to give you access to the whole property stock from the offices of any agent.

Agents work as "seller's agents" or "buyer's agents" and here is perhaps the most important piece of advice I can give you in this whole book:

You must recruit the services of a buyer's agent who has good experience working with British buyers.

Follow The Money

The real beauty of a buyer's agent is that you don't have to pay them!

The system works by having the seller pay their agent a commission for selling the property—and the seller's agent shares that commission with the buyer's agent. The possibility that they might get to keep all the commission is a strong motivation for a seller's agent to try and get you signed up to a deal without involving your own agent—regardless of how bad a deal it might be for you. That's why I kept saying earlier that it's a bad idea to follow up for sale signs, development promotions, property ads and so on—because they will all lead direct to a seller's agent.

Without a comprehensive understanding of the market, the property system and the *modus operandi* of these seller's agents, it is all too easy for an unsuspecting Brit to end up in a deal without even realising it.

Legal Responsibilities

The key difference between the actions of the two agents in a deal—the seller's agent and the buyer's agent—is where their legal responsibilities lie.

The seller's agent has a legal responsibility towards their client, and although there are obviously over-arching laws that cover business practices in general, they have no fiduciary duty of care towards you with regard to protecting your interests or giving you any advice.

Once you enter into an agreement with a buyer's agent however, they have fiduciary duties to you that include things like reasonable care, loyalty, confidentiality and full disclosure.

As you can see, your agent really should be your most trusted advisor when looking for a property. They can give you the benefit of all their experience, they know the local market, they know the legal and financial systems (including all the local variations), they're legally bound to give you good advice and they don't cost you anything!

However you must realise that all agents are not the same.

The Right Agent For You

You should be aware that the vast majority of agents in Florida are self-employed. Although some will obviously be in business using their own name as their trading name, most are more likely to be working within one of the very large nationally recognised real estate companies, within a franchise operation, or a local company.

Within these organisations, there is a fierce hierarchy of seniority—a pecking order of real estate agents—that can have serious implications for you as a buyer. For example, if you simply walk in off the street to a real estate office and sign up with an agent there, you will probably be dealing with a fairly junior agent who has to serve his time on the "shop floor" handling what are usually casual enquiries.

This is not the best person to act as your guide through the Florida property system! You are well advised instead to seek out specialised agents beforehand who understand your situation. It is especially important to find an agent to work with who understands the differences between the Florida and UK systems—how else can you expect them to highlight the critical differences where a simple assumption can turn into a costly mistake?

Your buyer's agent really is your best friend when buying a property in Florida, and they can guide you through the entire purchase process, including opening doors to finance, introducing you to other specialists and guiding you through all the legal processes. Make sure you choose this important ally wisely and you will reap the benefits in a hundred different ways.

CLOSING THE DEAL

It is of course impossible to talk completely about closing the deal on your Florida property without making sure the right finance is in place—and that's a big enough subject to justify a whole section of this book all to itself.

So, to let us follow the buying process through to its conclusion without getting too bogged down in the details of mortgages, currency transfers and so on, I'll cover some financial matters very broadly for now—and then return to them in detail in the next section.

The Deal Isn't Closed Until…

Purchasing a property in Florida has two key stages:
1. Once you have found the property you want, you will sign an agreement of sale. This commits both you and the seller to the deal, but usually only within the context of a number of conditions or clauses that you must both satisfy.
2. There are a number of contingencies that are commonly included, but you can include anything that is agreed by you and the seller. It is certainly common to make an offer contingent upon the outcome of the various inspections described later in this chapter, and you may make the sale conditional upon you getting the right kind of mortgage, or upon the seller providing appropriate documentation to prove ownership, and so on.
3. The final stage is "settlement" or "closing", and brings with it a significant range of different fees. We'll look at

these in more detail later, but a useful leaflet from the US Department of Housing and Urban Development contains full details of everything to account for—and handy tables to help you keep track of all the costs involved.

Time Is Of The Essence

This Is Important! In Florida, "time is of the essence" isn't just a saying—it's fundamental to the way contracts are written *and enforced*. Any commitment to action by a specific date is binding, and British buyers especially must pay careful attention to every date that is included in the contract. The most common areas where time is of the essence are:

- **Deposits**. In a typical contract the buyer will give a smallish deposit with the initial offer, with a second deposit due within a specific number of days. If you fail to get this second deposit to the appropriate party by the due date the seller could declare you in default and sell the property to another buyer.
- **Time to Accept the Offer**. If the contract is going back and forth between seller and buyer while price negotiation is taking place, both parties need to pay particular attention to the clause "Time for acceptance". If either party fails to meet these time scales the offer or counter offer could be withdrawn.
- **Mortgage/Financing Contingency**. If the contract is subject to mortgage financing be sure that both application and approval dates are realistic and adhered too.
- **Who is Responsible for Title Insurance?** If the seller is responsible for providing a title insurance commitment by a certain date and fails to deliver the buyer may well use this as a way out of the contract and claim default by the seller.
- **Property Inspections**. You typically have a very limited time frame to have your home inspections carried out. If

you do not complete these inspections within the given time frame you probably have lost that right and not only will you be unable to claim any compensation for repairs, you may be stuck buying a home that requires costly repairs you were unaware of.

If you don't meet each milestone as it comes up, the seller can pull out of the deal, and will probably keep any deposit you have already paid.

That might not be likely to happen if you have a motivated seller who is keen to sell to you, but in a "hot" area with rising prices, the current owner could have received a higher offer after your initial agreement of sale. Under these circumstances, they might look for any loophole to get out of the agreement—and date-related default is the most common way out.

Trusted Advisors

Before you can make a final commitment to a property, you need to enlist the support of a team of professionals who will protect your interests and avoid costly mistakes.

Mortgage Agent

There are many critical differences between how mortgages work in Florida and the USA, and there can be serious consequences if you get the wrong kind of mortgage for the property you buy—or the way you plan to use it.

We'll talk a lot more about mortgages in the next section, but suffice to say it's essential that you find an independent mortgage agent (also called mortgage brokers or mortgage planners) who understands and is experienced in your kind of purchase—second home, retirement property, investment property, etc—and works extensively with UK citizens buying in Florida.

Independent Appraiser

The job of the professional appraiser is to determine the "value" of a property by gathering and analysing information about the property and the surrounding area—their objective being to prevent you form paying too much for a property, and to prevent the lender from lending more money than a property is worth.

The concept of "value" in this context can have several meanings:

Market Value

Market value is the "most probable" price that a willing seller and a willing buyer will arrive at through negotiation. It assumes:

- Both parties are motivated
- Both parties are "market-aware", that is they are well-informed and well-advised of current values
- A reasonable time is allowed for other people to view the property
- Payment is by some "conventional" method—cash or mortgage
- Negotiation of the transaction is genuine, with both parties completely independent of each other with no relationship between them

There are however at least two different approaches that might be used to arrive at a "market" value.

Cost Approach Valuation

The cost approach to valuation assumes that value is based on a very down-to-earth model that assumes the price someone will pay for a property is based only on the land value, plus the cost of construction and an allowance for desirability, minus depreciation.

This type of approach to valuation is appropriate where you are buying a property for your own exclusive use.

Income Approach Valuation

The income approach to valuation is based upon the estimated net income from renting the property or the operation of another business type based upon the property itself (as opposed to simply operating out of the property).

In most cases, the amount a lender will advance on a property is based on the *lesser* of the asking price or the appraisal, so an income approach valuation may be essential to raise sufficient financing for a property in a competitive seller's market.

An appraiser will arrive at their valuation based on a number of physical factors:
- Condition both inside and out
- Room layout and floor plan design
- If the home has been updated and modernised
- Size (square footage)
- Measured dimensions (including garage and outbuildings)

The appraiser will usually only consider property that is "fixed" to the land, so swimming pools and tubs that are above ground and small sheds and so on without fixed foundations will not usually factor in the valuation. Bear that in mind from both a buyer and seller's point of view.

An appraiser also factors in information from a variety of sources, including the Multiple Listing Service, tax assessors' records, courthouse records, private interviews (if information cannot be found publicly), other appraisers and their personal knowledge of the area.

Home Inspector

An appraiser will look at the general condition of the building and contents, but only a home inspector will go into sufficient detail to give the property a full head to toe health report that includes things like the quality of the electrical wiring, the waste drainage and whether or not the garbage disposal works properly.

In all, most inspectors will report on over 35 different aspects of the property—all of them items that could cause major headaches if you don't find out about them until later, and all of them having a potential influence on the price you pay for the property.

The older the property, the more invaluable an inspection is, as only this report will tell you if the roof will need to be replaced in a couple of years, or the air conditioner, or the window frames, or any number of other potentially costly discoveries.

Home inspectors are not regulated to the same extend as other professionals you will use throughout your property purchase, so you should take extra steps to ensure the qualifications, experience and reliability of the person doing this job—references from other members of your "team" are probably the best way to track down a great home inspector.

...And More Reports

While you're getting an appraisal and a home inspection done on your dream property, if you want to sleep soundly at night you should probably get a survey and insect pest inspection done too.

Yes, another two sets of costs to factor in, but again, they can both save you a fortune later.

Survey

The survey will show you exactly what the facts are with regards to boundaries, and any factors such as easements and encroachments that may have been established during the tenure of previous owners. A survey will confirm that any extensions or improvements are all legal and above board (so you don't find out later you have to pull them down) and exactly what rights you—and others—have to the use of your property.

Pest Inspection

Termites are a significant pest in Florida, and lenders are very likely to require a pest inspection before confirming finance on a property.

While a home inspection might highlight any obvious or potential problem areas, only a detailed inspection from a specialist will give you a complete health report on the current pest status and any possible future problems.

Bad News?

What happens if one of the reports above produces some bad news about the property? It doesn't have to be the end of the dream, as you have a number of options open to you, depending on the type and scale of the problem.

- **Ignore it**. It is almost inevitable that one or more of these reports will highlight something negative, but it may be so minor that it has no practical bearing on your plans.
- **Get a discount**. If the scale of the problem can be well defined (no risk of hidden problems) and the cost of remedying can be established and agreed with the seller, you might simply agree a sum to be removed from the buying price.
- **They fix it**. If the problem is bigger—or there is the possibility that further underlying problems might be revealed or caused by the repair—you might agree to purchase the property *contingent* on the current owner having the problem fixed to an agreed standard within a certain timescale. That secures the property as long as the repair is done, but lets you get out of the deal if they drag their feet or don't do it properly.
- **Walk away**. Some problems are so significant that it is wiser simply to walk away rather than get too involved in trying to work out ways or prices at which you would still be interested in the property. There are plenty more out there!

Home Warranties

Although you might buy a home warranty yourself as part of your overall insurance and maintenance package, these are frequently offered by sellers to give buyers increased peace of mind.

Basically, home warranties take over where insurance stops—for example, a home warranty would replace a leaky hot water tank and your insurance would pay to redecorate the water damage caused by it.

Usually there is a core set of included items covered, then a menu of optional extras you can chose to cover. A typical home warranty in Florida will cover things like:

- Air Conditioning System
- Gas, Oil or Electric Heating
- Ductwork
- Plumbing and Polybutylene Pipe Leaks
- Water Heater
- Toilets
- Instant Hot Water Dispenser
- Water Pressure Regulator
- Sump Pump
- Recirculating Pump
- Built-in Bathtub Whirlpool Motor & Pump
- Dishwasher
- Kitchen Refrigerator
- Oven/Range/Hob/Cooker
- Garbage Disposal
- Built-in Microwave
- Trash Compactor
- Electrical System
- Exhaust and Ceiling Fans
- Central Vacuum
- Telephone Wiring

That list includes some pretty major domestic appliances and systems, with extra fees covering items such as:

- Swimming Pool, Spa and similar equipment
- Washing Machine/Dryer
- Blocked Drains
- Septic System
- Roof Leaks

Home warranties are usually renewed annually—so including one with the property is like the owner giving you a one year guarantee on the covered items. These policies don't usually limit the number of claims you can make within the year, except that there is typically a per-call charge payable to the specialist who attends.

Finally…

Finally closing the deal on your dream is a massive landmark—but don't forget it is also the beginning of your life as a property-owner in Florida, so make sure your plans and calculations have included all the ongoing costs that apply.

The calculation, application and payment of property taxes for example is very different from the Council Tax system in the UK, and it varies right down to the county and even city locality, so it's important you understand how this will apply to every property you consider buying—and that you factor the costs into your budget.

This takes me on rather nicely to all matters financial in the next section.

FINANCING PROPERTY IN FLORIDA

INTRODUCTION

At first glance, there are enough similarities in terminology to make Brits buying property in Florida think that the mortgage system will be quite easy to find their way round… so they can put that to one side for the moment and concentrate on finding a great property at the right price.

Wrong!

The one thing that every UK citizen buying in Florida *must* remember at every single stage of the process is to never make *any* assumptions about how things work in Florida. Yes, some differences are minor—but others might just make the difference between a successful purchase and disaster. You must remember that to the average person in Florida, the system they have is the only system in the world, so they will not be going out of their way to highlight any differences to you.

The only way to guarantee the success of your Florida property purchase is to arm yourself with as much factual information as possible—and get relevant advice from the right people. The "right people" in this context are people in the business who have specific experience of dealing with British clients looking for not just any mortgage in Florida, but the same type of mortgage you are looking for.

MORTGAGE TYPES

Many of the popular types of mortgage available to British citizens buying in Florida will generally be familiar—in particular the basic fixed rate and adjustable (variable) rate mortgages. However, there are many variations on these themes that have no real UK equivalents—as well as a whole raft of programs and offers that are really only suitable for special case USA citizens.

Fixed Rate Mortgages

These have traditionally been the most popular type of mortgage in Florida. With a fixed rate mortgage, you pay both capital and interest over a fixed period of (usually) 10,15,20 or 30 years at exactly the same monthly payment for the duration of the loan.

This suits people who value knowing exactly what their repayments are going to be over the long term and don't want to take any risk of being affected by rising interest rates.

Adjustable Rate Mortgages

Adjustable rate mortgages (like UK variable rate) in Florida usually have a fixed interest rate for the start of the term (typically one, three, five or seven years), after which the rate is adjusted either once every six months or once every year (depending on the mortgage) and fluctuates in line with independent published financial indexes.

There is a specific form of ARM that is proving very popular with people buying property in Florida—especially where rental income is involved. This "Option ARM" is covered separately below.

Interest Only Loans

Interest only loans are popular in Florida for investors or individuals who are looking at their property as a shorter-term investment. When you take out an interest only loan you are only paying the interest due and the total amount borrowed is still due at the end of the loan. This is the lowest payment you can make without actually increasing the amount owed.

"Equity Builder" Mortgage

These may have different names, but the underlying idea is instead of the normal monthly payments, a payment of approximately half that amount is paid every two weeks. The loan's 26 biweekly payments each year pay off a loan faster than 12 monthly payments and can save thousands of dollars in interest over the life of the loan compared to a similar 30-year monthly-payment mortgage.

Special Case Mortgages

You will sometimes see references to things like "piggyback" or "balloon" loans. These are just a couple of examples of a wide variety of special case mortgages that are designed to serve very particular circumstances. The construction of these loans can be quite complex, sometimes involving multiple loans that are related to each other, or highly front- or back-end weighted payment schedules.

Suffice to say that there is a mortgage structure for almost any situation, and once they understand your circumstances, your mortgage broker will almost certainly be able to find a suitable mortgage to fit the situation.

The Option ARM

The Option ARM (Adjustable Rate Mortgage) has a variable interest rate that fluctuates in line with independent published financial indexes just like a regular ARM.

The key difference is that each month your statement gives you typically four different payment options to choose from.

…and you actually get to choose which one you make.

There are some variations on the theme, but the most common payment options are:

- **Minimum Payment.** This is the lowest of the four payments and is like making the minimum payment on your credit card. With this payment you are paying neither the principal *nor* the entire amount of interest due on the loan. The interest that you leave unpaid this month *gets added back into the interest due on the loan* and this increases your actual loan balance.
- **Interest Only Payment.** This option is the second lowest payment type. With this payment you avoid deferring interest and increasing the amount of the loan (which is what the minimum payment does) but at the same time you are not actually reducing the amount of capital owed.
- **30-Year Payment.** Also called the "30-Year Fully Amortizing Payment", this is the equivalent of the payment that someone makes on their standard 30 year mortgage, going towards repaying both principal and interest. If you made this payment every month, you would pay off the loan in 30 years.
- **15-Year payment.** This is similar to the 30-year payment, but is an accelerated repayment option that would result in the loan being repaid in 15 years if you made this payment every month.

The idea is that you can modify your payment behaviour month by month as your circumstances dictate. The difference between the minimum payment and 15-year payment options can be around 100%—that is, the option of paying between $1000 and $2000.

Although the Option ARM is applicable to anyone who has a fluctuating income or who values the extra flexibility it offers in managing household finances, it is especially attractive to people with an investment portfolio (offering the flexibility of putting their money into higher yielding investments when the opportunity presents itself rather than tying it up in their mortgage)—and to people relying on rental income to pay the mortgage.

An Option Arm allows you to reduce your outgoings in the months when rental income is low—or when you have extra property-related costs to cover—and re-invest a bigger proportion of the income during the months of fuller occupancy.

This can be a massive help in managing a positive cash-flow as well as allowing you to finance minor emergencies without having to inject extra cash into the "Florida property" part of your bank account.

There are two possible "downsides" of an Option ARM:
- **Variable Rate.** There is a degree of risk associated with the interest rate being variable rather than fixed for the full term.
- **Management.** This is an active mortgage—you have to be prepared to study the monthly statement and make an active decision about what you are going to pay.

As well as the different types of mortgages available, it's important to understand that there are different types of mortgages depending on the use you plan for the property. There are certainly different rules for mortgages on properties as primary residence, second homes and as investments—and sometimes there are different or additional rules for foreign residents on top of those!

Mortgages For Rental Properties

You must ensure however, that you—and your advisers—are completely open about why you are buying a property in Florida, or it is very easy to fall into a trap that can have serious consequences.

For example, as you research the market, you may see advertisements featuring loans of up to 80% of the property value—an attractive proposition that may increase your buying power.

However, these loans are typically only available on properties that are for your personal occupation as a primary or secondary residence—and are specifically not offered on rental properties.

BUYING & SELLING PROPERTY IN FLORIDA
A UK RESIDENTS GUIDE

Some agents and brokers may be less than open about these factors until you are presented with the final documents to sign.

This can result in you being literally at the eleventh hour and closing on the property, with a difficult decision to make. Do you pull out of the deal and potentially lose the property (and your deposit) while you find a mortgage that is properly designed for your planned use, or do you sign a document you know to be false? The latter course should not really be up for consideration as the potential consequences are unthinkable—under Florida law, this would count as perjury.

That's a classic example of the need for an experienced mortgage broker who understands your situation—especially the fact that you are from the UK—and can guide you through the Florida mortgage system.

Getting the right type of mortgage can also be a consideration when you are signing the contract that commits you to purchasing a property. As I said before, it is common for such contracts in America to carry "contingencies"—which you can think of as "what-if's that might stop you going ahead with the purchase.

A number of contingencies are almost standard in such contracts, but if you are a British buyer of a property you plan to rent out—you need to have a special contingency in your contract that allows you to back out of the deal if you cannot get the type of investment mortgage you require for this purpose. Without that clause, you would be committed to either buying the property with a mortgage that doesn't allow you to rent it out, or perjuring yourself to mortgage the property as a primary or secondary home.

MORTGAGE MISCELLANEA

Mortgage Availability

With the correct guidance, getting a mortgage for a property in Florida is not normally a problem. You can even apply online in some cases!

Mortgages of up to 75% of the property value can usually be obtained by self-certification, which is a very straightforward process. Some brokers can give you a sliding scale range of choices depending on just how much documentation you can provide, but in general the more proof of past income and credit status you can provide...the lower your mortgage rate will be.

Larger mortgage percentages (smaller deposits) usually require proof not only of income, but of expenditure too—the lender gets more and more concerned about affordability at these levels.

Mortgage Affordability

The broad affordability calculation is similar to that used in the UK, with most people allowed to borrow 3.5 times the first income plus the second income.

While those figures may be relevant if you are buying a primary residence based on income, bear in mind that the affordability of an investment mortgage is based on the realistic income potential of the property as much as on your own income.

Break even calculations for rental properties are typically based on a maximum 70% mortgage—any more and you require occupancy levels that are unrealistic in most cases.

Pre-Approved Mortgages

A "pre-approved" mortgage means getting your mortgage

approved in principle before you go looking for a property—and it's a good idea to do this.

As well as giving you the confidence that you can afford to buy, the associated documentation will tell real estate brokers and their sellers that you are a serious buyer. In a business that works on commission and a fierce hierarchy of seniority within sales forces, this can open doors to levels of personal service and experience that isn't available to you if you simply walk in off the street with an enquiry.

Getting your mortgage application pre-approved also saves time in completing the mortgage application when you find the property you want. This can be important as—if you remember—"time is of the essence" is fundamentally true with Florida contracts. This is no time for last-minute hiccups in getting your mortgage arranged!

Stay Approved

Bear in mind that pre-approval is granted conditionally, based on the facts *at that time*. The lender reserves the right to check those facts again at any time, and it isn't unusual for them to run a second check immediately before closing.

So, you should be careful not to do anything between pre-approval and closing that seriously affects your credit-worthiness in the eyes of the lender.

Extra Debt. Taking on any additional debts will affect your debt to income ratio adversely—a major credit purchase like a car may raise a red flag on your credit report.

Stable Money. The balances of all your accounts are recorded during the pre-approval process. Large withdrawals (or deposits) in any of those accounts—or closing accounts—may raise a red flag.

Stable Employment. Moving to a regular salary job of equal or higher pay should be ok, but a drop in income—or any job move where some income is based on variables like commission or bonuses—may be a problem.

Dollar or Sterling Mortgage?

As well as the interest rate that is built-in to your mortgage, the exchange rate between the pound and the dollar will have a bearing on the true cost of financing your home—unless of course you have moved completely to Florida and deal only in dollars.

Having an asset (your Florida home) that is valued in dollars while at least part of your income is in sterling will inevitably expose you to the vagaries of fluctuating exchange rates. Sometimes the pounds you get for renting the home to other UK residents will pay a lot of the mortgage, other times your dollar costs will seem more expensive when you have to transfer pounds to pay them.

It is virtually impossible to eliminate all possible currency risk for as long as you have an interest in both currencies, so any decision you make concerning mortgaging in dollars or sterling will at best influence the degree of that risk and whether you ride the fluctuations in exchange rates throughout the life of the mortgage—or roll up all your risk until you sell the house.

As a very general rule, you are likely to be better off with a US mortgage in dollars, but this is an area where you are well advised to consult with mortgage advisers who understand the needs of UK citizens mortgaging in Florida *plus* your personal circumstances.

All The Fees

There are a large number of different fees payable in the process of "closing" (completing) on the purchase of property in Florida. These fees become due at different times and are payable to different people, so there is a lot of potential for confusion—and for buyers to misunderstand the full costs involved.

Good Faith Estimates

Fortunately, there are programs in place in the USA to clarify this confusion and to promote "truth in lending". When shopping for a mortgage, you should ensure you are given a "fully disclosed Good Faith Estimate" and/or a HUD-1 disclosure. The HUD-1 is the more formal of these (HUD is the Department of Housing and Urban Development) and there are some providers who will omit some closing fees from their "good faith" estimates so they can show a lower overall price.

You must be aware that the exclusion of these fees from an estimate will not prevent them being charged at closing, so make sure that your estimates include all the fees below—or an explanation for their omission.

Fees Set By	Fees	Negotiable?
Loan Servicer	Appraisal Fee Tax Service Fee Document Prep Fee Underwriting Fee Credit Report Fee Survey Pest Inspection Escrow Waiver Fee Flood Determination Mortgage Insurance	Ask your broker what can be reduced or eliminated from these fees – and how.
Closing Agent/Title Company	Settlement/Closing Fee Abstract/Title Search Title Insurance Title Endorsements Lenders Policy Simultaneous	Discounts are available from industry standard fees.

	Issue Courier/Fed-Ex	
State & Local Taxes	State Tax Intangible Tax Recording Fees City/County Tax	These taxes are fixed – they cannot be reduced.
Broker	Broker Fee Processing Fee Origination Fee Discount Points	Ask your broker what can be reduced or eliminated from these fees.

How To Reduce Fees

Some of these fees can be offset by higher mortgage interest rates——so if you have limited start-up funds but are willing and able to sustain higher monthly payments, this may be an option to consider. It might make sense if you plan to resell the property quickly——or if you must protect your capital for other start-up costs——but most buyers appreciate a lower interest rate over many years rather than saving a few dollars at the beginning

…And How Not To

Making a conscious decision to pay a higher interest rate as a trade-off against some benefit that you value——like lower up-front costs—under special circumstances is one thing, but don't get duped into paying higher rates by smart marketing and deceptive advertising.

No-one likes paying these closing costs——and the fact that there are so many individual items makes it seem even worse. There are companies out there who have realised this, and their sharp practices could cost you a fortune.

These companies hide the closing costs under the heading of "free" loans, but you don't have to be a genius to know that the closing costs are still there and someone is still paying them—so how is this loan "free" from closing costs.

The answer of course is in the interest rate. Because we are dealing with mortgage loans here, where the amounts are large and the length of the loan is long, it only takes a small increase in interest rate to generate a substantial sum in additional income for the loan provider. For example, by increasing the interest rate by "only" 0.375% (which doesn't sound like much, does it?):

Loan value:	**$200,000**
Interest over 10 years at market rate of 6%:	**$111,263**
Interest over 10 years at 6.375%:	**$118,746**
Extra interest paid:	**$7,483**

Does it seem like a good deal to pay an extra $7,483 over the life of the loan to avoid say $3000 in closing fees? Even if you have very special circumstances that mean you don't want to pay the $3000 up-front, I suggest you can probably find a cheaper way to finance the closing fees than by signing up for one of these "free" loans.

TAXING CONCERNS

The first thing to say with regard to taxes is that they are very personal things. Although there are some broad guidelines I can give here about taxes to be aware of, the impact of those taxes on you as an individual will vary according to your exact circumstances.

How you operate your financial affairs between the UK and the USA, residency status, the path your money follows in and out of the country will all have a potential bearing on your tax liabilities—and any opportunities to minimise your taxes will be dependent upon exact circumstances, not broad generalisations!

Bottom line: get good professional advice from people who understand all the ins and outs of tax for UK owners of Florida property. Everyone in the USA is required to submit (file) an annual tax return, and over half of them use some kind of help in preparing that return—not always a qualified professional accountant.

Assuming you have not moved all your financial affairs within the borders of the USA, you would be well advised to get the help of someone familiar with international finance to help file your tax return.

I will include some indicative figures in this chapter purely to put my comments in context—you will of course be aware that things like rates and allowances can be changed by local and federal government at any time.

If you want to do some in-depth research of your own in advance, the up-to-date technical details can be found online at the websites of the Inland Revenue Service (www.IRS.gov) and the Florida Department of Revenue (www.MyFlorida.com/dor).

Resident Or Not?

Depending on what residency status you have (if any), you may be taxed as a resident or a non-resident. If you're a permanent resident of the US or a US citizen, you must file a tax return that includes all your worldwide income.

Non-residents are taxed only on income that is US-sourced—the most obvious regular candidates being rental income and any other income arising from your property ownership.

Tax On Income

All rental income received in Florida is subject to US tax and is paid locally. The first piece of good news is that tax treaties between the USA and the UK mean you won't have to pay tax twice on income earned in the USA.

The next piece of good news (you thought a chapter on taxes was going to be all bad news didn't you?) is that Florida is one of the few states in the USA that don't impose personal income tax—a luxury that the state affords mainly due to the substantial volumes of sales tax generated by the tourist industry. You do however still have to pay federal income tax.

Federal income tax is not very dissimilar to the UK at lower levels, but it is more generous as your income gets higher—with a large 20% band and a maximum rate of 35% that doesn't kick in until considerably higher than the UK higher rate.

In practice, many property rental experts suggest that you should expect to pay little or no tax on rental income. This is because the taxable allowances for this activity are extremely generous and include your mortgage interest, maintenance and other fees and costs, plus an allowance for two annual "inspection" flights from the UK.

Sales Tax

Florida businesses must collect sales tax for many products and services—the complete list is at the Florida Department of Revenue website. You must register initially as a sales tax dealer and then pay the sales tax you collect to the state on a monthly basis—unless you are collecting relatively small amounts, in which case you may pay quarterly, twice yearly, or even annually.

Your management company will probably include the collection of this tax in their service.

Use Tax

"Use" Tax is a novel concept for Brits moving to Florida, and comes about because of the different local sales tax rates from state to state.

Although there are some complex rules concerning special cases, the general idea is that if you buy a product in one state (or another country) and bring it into Florida to *use* it, then you have to pay tax on it as if it were purchased within the state. If the state you purchased from has already applied some sales tax, you only pay use tax at a level that brings the total tax paid up the total amount you would have paid if purchased in Florida.

Again, it is likely that your liability for any use tax will be for products and services routed through your management company—and they will of course be much more familiar with the concept than you are!

INSURANCE

Insurance is a critical element that has to be included in your financial calculations regarding a Florida property.

There are a number of different insurances that will be more or less important depending on your circumstances.

Homeowners Insurance

This is the most important insurance wrapper, covering what would normally be separate buildings and content cover in the UK.

When you take out homeowners insurance, make sure you insure for the total amount it would cost to rebuild your property if it were destroyed, and to replace your possessions. If you don't have sufficient insurance, your insurance company may only pay a portion of the cost of replacing or repairing damaged items.

There are three main ways to insure the structure of your home:

- **Replacement Cost.** Insurance that pays the cost of replacing the damaged property up to an agreed limit but without any deduction for depreciation.
- **Guaranteed Replacement Cost.** Insurance that pays the full cost of replacing damaged property, without a deduction for depreciation and without a dollar limit. This coverage is not available in all states and some companies limit the coverage to 120% of the expected cost of rebuilding your home. One of the uses of this type of insurance is to provide protection against a sudden increase in construction costs due to a shortage of building

materials following a natural catastrophe—which do happen in Florida.
- **Actual Cash Value.** Insurance that pays an amount equal to the replacement value of damaged property minus an allowance for depreciation. Note—unless your policy *specifies* that property is covered for its replacement value, you can assume the cover is for actual cash value.

Local real estate appraisers and builders' associations keep track of a key figure—the "local building cost"—for different house types. Multiplying this by the total square footage of your house gives you a quick estimate of the cost of rebuilding your home to make sure you are adequately insured.

This rough figure has to be combined with additional factors to get a more accurate cost:
- Type of exterior wall construction
- Style of the house (ranch, colonial, etc)
- Number of rooms
- Number of bathrooms
- Type of roof
- Attached garages, fireplaces, exterior trim
- Special features like arched windows

You should check the value of your insurance policy against rising local building costs each year. Ask your insurance agent or company representative about adding an "Inflation Guard Clause" to your policy. This automatically adjusts the limit when you renew your policy to reflect current construction costs in your area. Also, be sure to increase the limit of your policy if you make improvements or additions to your house.

How To Save Money on Homeowners Insurance
Shop Around

Friends, family, the phone book and Internet are some of the sources you can use to find homeowners insurers. Get a wide range of prices from several companies, but don't consider price alone. The insurer you select should offer both a fair price and excellent service. Quality service may cost a bit more, but you really appreciate it when you have an insurer you can depend on in an emergency.

Don't Shop Around!

Some companies that sell other insurances—such as car and liability insurance—will take 5-15% off your premium if you buy two or more policies from them.

Raise Your Deductible

Deductibles are the amount of money you have to pay toward a loss before your insurance company starts to pay. Deductibles on homeowners policies typically start at $250 and you can save 10-30+% on the policy depending on how much you are willing to pay per claim.

Hurricane Deductible

You should be aware that there is a law in Florida that establishes a special-case relationship between hurricane deductibles and policy discounts. About 70% of Florida homeowners take advantage of a system that gives them a discount on the wind-related portion of their policy in return for accepting a special deductible for hurricane related damage that amounts to 2% of the policy limits.

Buy With Insurance In Mind

When looking at potential properties to purchase, consider how much they will cost to insure. A new home's electrical, heating and plumbing systems and overall structure are likely to be in better shape than those of an older house. Insurers may offer you a discount of 8-15% if your house is new. Check the home's construction; is it the best choice for the area? The closer your house is to the local firehouse or other major fire fighting equipment...the lower your premium will be.

Insure The House, Not The Land

The land under your house isn't at risk from theft, wind, storm, fire and the other risks covered in your homeowners policy. So don't include its value in deciding how much homeowners insurance to buy. If you do, you'll pay a higher premium than you should.

Improve Home Security And Safety

You can usually get discounts of at least 5% for a smoke detector, burglar alarm, or dead-bolt locks. Some companies offer to cut your premium by as much as 15-20% if you install a sophisticated sprinkler system and a fire and burglar alarm that rings at the police station or other monitoring facility. These systems aren't cheap and not every system qualifies for the discount. Before you buy such a system, find out what kind your insurer recommends, how much the device would cost...and exactly how much you'd save on premiums.

Stop Smoking

Smoking accounts for more than 23,000 residential fires a year. That's why some insurers offer to reduce premiums if all the residents in a house don't smoke.

Act Your Age

Retired people stay at home more and spot fires sooner than working people and have more time for maintaining their homes. If you're at least 55 years old and retired, you may qualify for a discount of up to 10% at some companies.

Be Loyal

If you've kept your coverage with a company for several years, you may receive special consideration. As well as straightforward loyalty discounts, "no-claims" discounts may be available too.

Review Your Limits

You want your policy to cover any major purchases or additions to your home, but equally there is no point insuring items that you no longer own, use or value...or that have depreciated to the point where you couldn't claim anything for them. Don't spend money for coverage you don't need.

Title Insurance

Title insurance protects your ownership right to your home both from fraudulent claims against your ownership that arise after you have bought it, and from title-related mistakes made in earlier sales. These might include a mistake in the spelling of a person's name or an inaccurate description of the property. Worst case, title insurance protects you in case it is subsequently discovered that someone in your home's history didn't actually have the right to sell it. Yes, it happens!

Title insurance is a one-time cost, paid as part of the closing package and usually based on the price of the property. Taking out such a policy will trigger a thorough search of the appropriate public records relating to the property to establish the current status of the title.

There are separate policies for owners and for lenders. An owner's policy protects only the owner while a mortgage policy protects only the holder of the mortgage on the property. Separate policies are required to protect both interests, but special rates are often available when both owners and mortgage policies are applied at the same time.

Title insurance is often cheaper if the home has been bought within only a few years since not as much work is required to check the title.

Flood Insurance

Flooding (including storm surge from a hurricane, which is considered flooding) is not covered by a standard homeowners insurance policy.

To determine if you need flood insurance, ask your insurance professional, mortgage company or neighbours about the flood history in your area. If there is a potential for flooding, you should consider purchasing a policy that covers the structure and your personal belongings.

Flood insurance is only available where the local government has adopted adequate flood plain management regulations under the National Flood Insurance Program (NFIP), and not having flood cover where required will count as being under-insured (see above), resulting in under-payment of a claim that includes several elements including flood damage.

MONEY MATTERS

Moving on to consider some of the issues surrounding the actual handling of hard cash while buying, owning and selling Florida properties...

US Bank Accounts

Do you need a Bank Account in the USA?

Yes—you will certainly need a US bank account to get a US mortgage, and it will of course be the most convenient way to handle the financial ins and outs associated with managing your Florida property month to month.

The main thing you have to be aware of as a foreigner in this context is that there is likely to be a great deal of suspicion associated with non-residents opening US bank accounts. Indeed, the Patriot Act added so many new hurdles that if you simply walk in off the street, many banks will not offer you an account—many believe it to be impossible anyway!

It isn't impossible—but it will be much more straightforward if you get an introduction to a specific branch or individual within a branch from one of your advisers such as your real estate agent or mortgage representative.

It is a good idea to simply open the account with a few hundred dollars cash—walking in with a briefcase full of cash will not help counter any fears that you are an international criminal—then transfer larger amounts through the banking system as required.

Currency Conversion

If you are buying a property in Florida, you will inevitably have to pay in US Dollars.

Buying "off plan" means you will have to pay an immediate deposit followed by several "stage payments" as construction progresses and a final payment upon completion.

The amounts of money that are likely to be involved—and the fact that they may be spread over 18 months while your house is built—mean that how and when you convert your money from Sterling to Dollars can play a key role in your property transactions. What may seem like relatively small fluctuations in the published exchange rates can in fact be a percentage shift that translates into thousands of pounds when multiplied up by the scale of the typical property purchase.

For example, a move in the exchange rate from 1.70 to 1.785 is a 5% change—saving you £5000 on a £100,000 house purchase.

However, you don't have to play the currency markets (which can of course go up as well as down) to make all your currency transactions as cost-effective as possible.

You can obviously walk into any high street bank or bureau de change and exchange your currency for Dollars. This may be convenient for your holidays but for larger amounts of currency it pays to deal with a specialist foreign exchange company. Specialist brokers deal exclusively in high-volume transactions and their overheads are much lower, resulting in a better deal for you:

- More competitive exchange rates
- The ability to "fix" exchange rates for long periods
- Fast international money transfers
- No commission charges
- Professional information (currency dealers are not regulated to give you "advice" in the same way that other financial professions are)

Currency dealers make a margin on your money from the high-volume rates they obtain in the money markets, and in general the more money you wish to convert the better the rate. You will often have one or more transaction fees to pay—and it is worth double checking these as it is not impossible to end up paying fees to your UK bank, the currency dealer and your US bank on each transaction.

This is why it is always wise to look at the total cost of transferring an amount rather then getting too fixated on the exchange rate.

Once you have set up a client account, you can usually set up regular payments—for mortgages, management fees, etc—via your foreign exchange dealers, and the ability to fix the exchange rate at which these payments are made can be very useful when budgeting. Some dealers will let you fix rates up to two years ahead. For "off plan" purchases in particular, this means you can fix the cost of your home on day one, regardless of any currency fluctuations that occur during its construction.

When you are close to making a large purchase, you can—if you want—play the currency market by setting a target rate at which you would like to make the transfer to your US bank. On the other hand, if you think today's rate is as good as it's going to get but you don't need to transfer the cash right now—you can "forward buy" your currency by making a deposit payment at today's rate and thereby securing that rate for the full transfer value at a later date.

Escrow Accounts

Escrow is a concept that most British buyers are unfamiliar with, but in the Florida real estate system you will come across it in two different contexts; as a mechanism to hold deposits when buying property, and as a way to securely combine tax and insurance with your mortgage payments.

In practice, a third party escrow agent is retained by two parties to act as a trusted "middle man" during the transfer of valuable items under agreed conditions.

When closing on the purchase of a home, the escrow agent holds the buyer's deposit and various documents that are provided by each party. They ensure that all the terms and conditions of the sales agreement have been fulfilled, and only when everything is in place will they disburse funds and documents to their final destinations.

Using escrow means that each party can proceed with fulfilling their obligations to the agreement, secure in the knowledge that their deposit (or property) is not at risk—it will only be released under predetermined and agreed circumstances.

Escrow agents will fiercely maintain their independence of both parties and will not offer any advice. They are completely bound by procedure, so make sure you understand exactly what they require of you. The most commonly made mistake is to try and give an escrow agent funds that are in the wrong format—they will not accept cash if they have specified bank transfer, for example.

The other type of escrow account is associated with mortgages—and is a useful convenience. A Mortgage Escrow Account is usually established and partially funded during closing, and acts as a fund from which your mortgage lender will pay recurring expenses such as property taxes and home insurance.

Each month, you make a contribution to these costs as part of your mortgage payment—and the escrow account holds the portion that doesn't belong to the lender. Then, as annual insurance or other costs fall due, they get the money from the escrow account and pay them on your behalf.

Using escrow in this context means your funds are secure and protected from fraudulent access—or even from your lender going out of business.

MANAGING A HOME IN FLORIDA

INTRODUCTION

One of the most common reasons for buying a property in Florida is to use it as a holiday home and finance the purchase through rentals to other holidaymakers throughout the year.

Once you have a property in Florida, you have to decide how you will handle the management of all the issues surrounding renting it out if that is your intention.

Unless you are living not only in Florida, but close to your rental property—and have the time, energy and knowledge necessary to take care of all this yourself—you will probably use the services of a management company.

As this company will be the interface between you and your tenants, and indeed for much of the time will be the interface between you and your own property, it is clear that the selection of the right company and the right services are critical to the success of this enterprise.

Pick the right company and the right set of services and you will be able to enjoy the benefits of Florida property ownership without any of the headaches—even when you are thousands of miles away from your investment.

In this section we'll look at the economics of property rental, some of the business-related matters you need to consider, how a management company can help with your property—and how to find the right company for your needs.

THE ECONOMICS OF RENTAL

I make references to renting out your Florida property throughout this book, but I thought it would be worthwhile in this section to answer a few common questions and clear up some common misconceptions about the economics of the rental business.

The Economics Of Property Rental

Financing an "investment" property is viewed somewhat differently from the purchase of a primary home—mainly because lenders understand that these properties rely on rental income to pay the mortgage and consequently there is a degree of commercial risk involved.

In practice, this means that you will typically have to pay a bigger down payment (deposit) and the 80% or higher mortgages you will see advertised are simply not offered on these types of properties. Although this seems like a hurdle they are putting in front of you, it is in fact probably a kindness, because the economics of property rental mean that breaking even requires decent occupancy rates, controlled management costs and a sensible mortgage. Depending on all the other factors, a mortgage of 60% is a good target, 75% probably the maximum you should consider.

As we will see later, there are many variables, but the line between profit and loss can be very thin. This may not be critically important if you place a high value on your own use of the property, but if you need income to finance the purchase, you have to be passionate about managing the cost of every aspect of the purchase process.

Guaranteed Rental Income

With the sums of money and distances involved, advertised promises of "Guaranteed Rental Income" or "Guaranteed Return on Investment" can seem very appealing.

Too good to be true? All too often, unfortunately, yes.

Guaranteed income schemes do exist, but you have to look carefully at the full details of the offer and the motivation of the advertiser to fully understand what you are getting into.

First off, most guarantee income offers are short term and are used as a sales aid. Yes, it can be very useful to get a guaranteed income for (say) the first two years while you find your feet and get organised with regard to securing bookings, managing the property and so on.

However, you must think beyond those first two years and be sure that you are paying the right price for the property and that it ticks all the boxes for location, rentability and everything else. In short, if the property doesn't make sense without the guaranteed income offer, that short-term guarantee should not be the deciding factor.

In other cases, the guarantee may be subject to all kinds of terms and conditions that limit your choice of property, sales agents, mortgage, management company, rental rates and more. You can end up so hogtied by conditions that the property hardly feels like it belongs to you—the guarantee probably only scrapes you into break-even territory, and you can only use it for two weeks a year in mid-November!

Slim Margins

I talk in several places in the book about the different variables that influence the economics of investment properties, but the last point I will make for the moment is to illustrate the narrow margin between profit and loss in this field.

With a 60% mortgage, you might find that the break-even point is around 30 weeks per year occupancy, with a 75% mortgage that might be 35 weeks. Most people agree that 38-40 weeks is the best possible occupancy rate you can hope to achieve—the upper limits of which would give you something like 6% yield on your investment with a 75% mortgage. That's a lot resting on what might only be two bookings per year.

MANAGEMENT COMPANIES

There are literally thousands of management companies across Florida—several hundred of them in the Orlando area alone—so how do you find the right one amongst all that choice?

...and getting the right one is important as there are many companies appearing and disappearing every week (sometimes with money belonging to both tenants and owners) and a massive variety in the range of services and service levels offered.

Before You Start

The first thing is to make some decisions about what you need and want out of the relationship.

Rental Options

Consider what type of rental you are aiming for—each has its advantages and disadvatages and will have a bearing on the type of management company—and the range of services—you require.

Long Term Rentals

Long term rentals are usually for a year at a time. There are some advantages to long term rentals:
- Property can be let unfurnished
- 100% occupancy for long periods
- Less admin to worry about

On the other hand, a long term rental means you cannot use the property yourself—except between annual tenancies—and the rent levels are significantly lower for longer lets.

The management company you select for this type of rental

really only needs to find you tenants—you could use them on a reduced contract, or a separate local service company, to carry out maintenance and small repairs.

Short Term Rentals

The definition of short term rental in zoning restrictions is from a period of one day upwards. You can rent for any period longer than this—so you can promote a property for short term rental and still accept a long term rental if it comes along and the arrangement suits you.

For short term rentals you will need a much more involved management company with a wide range of services to ensure they can deal with everything you and your tenants need handled 24 hours a day, seven days a week.

Who Does What?

The next major question is to decide just how much time and effort you are willing and able to spend on managing your property. It's unlikely that it will be practical for you to get involved in the day-to-day or inter-let management, but there are some areas you might do yourself.

The main activity that many owners want to be more involved in is the process of marketing the property and finding tenants. This can be quite practical if you are marketing to UK holiday makers for example, as you are clearly in a good position to deal with UK advertising from home. The increasing use of the Internet can make it quite cost effective to promote a property through multiple sites.

On the other hand, you have to be aware of the competition, and many holiday makers find their holiday homes through companies who can offer them a wide selection of different properties to choose from, and it may be difficult for you as an individual to get your one property noticed against this kind of marketing budget.

Management companies are likely to marketing a large number of properties, so you get the benefits of the economies of scale and co-operative marketing—which means that they may get an enquiry that is initially for a property that turns out to be unsuitable or unavailable, and go on to convert that into a booking for you.

Choosing A Management Company

I'll go on to look at just what services companies might offer—and obviously it's important you find a company who offers the services you need at a fair price.

However, with the large number of companies involved and the occasional horror stories that we hear from this sector, there are some general checks you should do to establish that a property management company is worth even thinking about doing business with.

- **Experience.** It is perhaps unfair to dismiss new companies lightly—after all, everyone has to start somewhere—but dealing with a new management company can be very risky.
- It is not very difficult or expensive to set up a business of this type—making it a popular vehicle for people trying to get work or investor visas to the USA. This low barrier to entry also means that many companies set up without being fully funded or with a complete understanding of everything the business entails. This all leads in turn to a high turnover in management companies popping up and then soon after going out of business.
- Your management company will have access to an extremely valuable asset and probably significant amounts of cash that belong to you—this is not an area to take a risk in!
- **Performance.** There are a number of annual owner surveys published in the specialist press that report on the performance of management companies in Florida. This is an invaluable way to see what other owners have experienced.

- **Background**. You should confirm the status and credentials of a potential business partner like a management company with the local Better Business Bureau, Chamber of Commerce, Sheriff's office and any appropriate licensing authorities for the area. An Internet search for *"company name* +problems" can sometimes throw up interesting material—though you have to remember with such personal anecdotes that there are always two sides to every story.
- **Independence**. Watch out for management companies that are tied to developers or real estate companies. They may well have conflicting loyalties and there are stories of such partnerships working in collusion to use client's properties to provide free accommodation for new customer buying trips.
- **Recommendation**. If you have (as advised) been dealing with sales agents, mortgage brokers and so on who have specific experience of UK citizens buying property to rent out in Florida, it is likely that they can give some well-informed recommendations. Ideally, they will give you several companies to put on your shortlist based on feedback from other owners, so you can be sure they have an arms-length relationship with the companies and have no vested interest in you signing up with any one in particular.
- **References**. Always ask for references and always follow them up.

Property Management Services

Although individual companies may only offer specific services, or package them up into different service levels with catchy names, if you put them all together you will see there is a massively wide range of different services available for the property owner to choose from—and many companies will effectively offer you a menu to choose from so you can agree your own custom package.

Some of these services are more applicable to short-term rentals or long-term rentals, but in all cases remember—*you* are the customer here, and you should make sure you get the services you want…and that you don't pay for services you don't want.

Below, I list the main headings for property management services, along with the kinds of services you should discuss with potential partners:

- **Find tenants**. Promote your property through various media, carry out checks on potential tenants, manage the move-in and move-out cycle.
- **Collect rent**. Take payments reliably, collect debts, guarantee tenancy/payments/income, manage tenant security deposits.
- **Day-to-day maintenance and repairs**. Encourage tenant care, manage third party services, provide in-house services, operate within agreed limits.
- **Inspect and report**. Carry out move-in/out inspections, document/photograph/video inspections, provide maintenance and repair reports.
- **Accounting**. Provide monthly statements, quarterly/annual summaries, tax reporting, provide access to owner account, operate escrow or trust accounts, make payments on owner's behalf.
- **Handle problems and emergencies**. Provide tenant support services in person/online/telephone, manage and report on incidents.

Propert Management Costs

While I appreciate it would be useful to give an indication of costs for property management services here, the truth is that there are so many variables that it is impossible to give a meaningful figure—even as a percentage of rental income.

One thing you can be sure of is that the Florida property

management market is a very crowded and competitive one, so there is massive pressure on companies to improve efficiency and service levels while competing on price. The kind of percentage you might pay a company simply for referrals and booking services on a villa in another part of the world can get you a nice little portfolio of management services in Florida.

Clearly, the system works for thousands of rental property owners—and it will work for you if you do your homework and ensure you get exactly the right service package for your situation.

THE BUSINESS OF PROPERTY RENTAL

The relationship you strike up with your management company—and your personal circumstances—will define just how much you get personally "hands-on" involved in the business aspects of renting your property.

At one extreme you might hand over almost everything but ownership to the management company and simply account for the income and costs in your annual tax return. Or you might create your own company as a vehicle for your property rental activities and route everything through that.

Proper legal and financial advice is the only way to be sure what is right for you, but there are of course some extra issues to address as you move along the scale from private individual to business operator.

Dealing With The State

Florida is a very business-friendly state, but that does not mean it isn't also highly regulated.

Fortunately, Florida has worked very hard at making the mechanics of government accessible to its citizens, a philosophy that has also been adopted by many businesses in the state.

This is especially useful in our context because it means that not only is there a great deal of official information available on the internet, but you can also usually download and print the forms you need—indeed, you can often file applications and records directly with state departments and independent bodies online.

This is immensely useful in dealing with the official aspects of doing business in Florida—from your home or office in the UK.

The main web portal to the state administration is MyFlorida.com. There is a complete business portal within the site where you can access all the state agencies. Many of the key departments have their own portals—like the Florida Department of Business and Professional Regulation at MyFloridaLicense.com where you can check the status and qualifications of potential suppliers online.

Insurance Matters

If you are renting out your property, you should examine the additional cover you require to cover the business aspect of your property ownership. Exactly who may be liable for what may vary according to the details of the relationship you have with your management company and the people who rent your house. It may well be that your management company carries all the extra insurance necessary to cover you.

...but—especially given the increasingly litigious nature of people today—do take the time to clarify exactly who is liable for all the different scenarios that may occur.

- **General Liability Insurance.** General liability insurance may be required to cover you for personal injury claims from people on your property.
- **Business Interruption Insurance.** Also called business income insurance, this insurance compensates you for income lost due to another insured event.
- This is the insurance that would compensate you for the loss of rental income while your homeowners insurance pays to have the property repaired for example.
- **Umbrella Insurance.** Claims against general liability policies in particular can sometimes run into millions of dollars these days—more than typical policy limits.
- Umbrella insurance is an economical way to simply increase the amount covered by these policies.

SELLING A HOME IN FLORIDA

INTRODUCTION

No matter how much you love your Florida property, there will almost inevitably come a time when you want to sell it.

Circumstances might dictate a return to the UK, you may want to trade up to a bigger property or one in another area—or you might simply decide to "cash out" and realise the profit from your investment.

Whatever the reason for selling, there are (as you will have guessed by now) significant differences between the UK and Florida real estate systems as they apply to house sales.

At least now you have seen these from the buyer's point of view and you will be familiar with many aspects of the process. Indeed, so many of the important things about the buy/sell transaction have already been covered in the "buying" section that I suggest you read that first if you haven't already done so—because here I'll look at the process specifically from the seller's perspective.

Why Are You Selling?

Just as I asked you to do when we first looked at buying a property in Florida, I suggest first that you have a long hard think about what you want or need to achieve in selling it. This may have a significant bearing on a number of factors—especially in relation to time and money.

Your priorities and concerns if you are selling this property to move up or down the Florida market are likely to be quite different from those in place if you are selling to release the funds to return to the UK.

Everyone has a different balance of pressures upon them when selling, and it is very much a balancing act to decide the best plan. There are however three main situations:

1. **Do you want/need to get the maximum price?**
2. If so, are you willing to have your house on the market for a long time?
3. **Do you want/need to sell quickly?**
4. If so, are you willing to sacrifice some of your potential profits to achieve this?
5. **Would you like to achieve a balance**
6. …between selling your house quickly and getting the best price?

TIMING

Firstly, if you have the flexibility to choose; spring and autumn are the peak times for houses to sell, and autumn can be especially good for the sale of rental properties as there tend to be a few more people who have visited Florida over the summer and turn their thoughts to owning rather than renting again.

In an ideal world, you would sell one house and buy another on the same day, but that probably isn't going to happen. It pays to be prepared for how the timing is likely to work out in the real world, and seek where possible to influence it as you negotiate the two halves of the buying/selling equation.

In general, it's easier to manage a gap between homes than it is to finance two mortgages. Get a short-term lease, find temporary housing or stay with friends—anything is better than paying two mortgages at the same time!

If you are shopping for a new property before you have sold your own, remember that the people who buy your property will probably have to borrow to finance the purchase—and their lender will lend an amount based on the lower of the sales price or appraised value. If you get your own appraisal done, this will give you a more confident feel for how much money you have to spend on your next property—and prevent you from getting too attached to a property outside your buying power.

It's a good idea to get pre-approved for a mortgage on your next home as early as possible. Then, if you make a quick sale on your current property you won't be left waiting for approval before you can get serious about buying a new home.

If you have a buyer for your current property but haven't found a new home yet, you might be able to negotiate a long escrow period or a "sale and lease back" arrangement whereby you pay to stay in the house for a period after the sale. This probably isn't worth jeopardising a deal over though, so be prepared to look for temporary housing if the new owners want to take possession soon after closing.

If the opposite happens and you find yourself seriously interested in a new property before you have sold your current home, you could try the same arrangement in reverse. If the owner isn't in a hurry to move—and especially if the market is slow—they may well entertain it.

Managing carefully timed closing dates between a simultaneous sale and purchase might be possible if you are staying in the same area, but it gets a lot more difficult if you are moving away from Florida. Some documents can be faxed, and some can even be signed in the UK in front of an approved notary, but many will have to be couriered around the country or even across the Atlantic to finalise deals. Fortunately, your agent(s) can take a lot of the strain out of this process by helping co-ordinate the paperwork.

The best insurance against timing problems when buying and selling is…cash. Having a cash reserve that will fund your commitments for two or three months minimum is highly recommended, and will probably avoid the need for a bridging loan—an expensive alternative. Short term bridging loans, temporary accommodation and storage costs can quickly eat into the profit you make from the increase in your property's value, so it is always worth the effort to try and get your buying and selling closing dates as close as possible.

FOR SALE BY OWNER

For Sale By Owner (FSBO) describes people who sell their property themselves and don't use the services of a real estate company.

Like the growth in DIY conveyancing in the UK, FSBO represents a growing trend as many people are demonstrating their self-reliance rather than pay the commission fees of 6% or so that real estate agents or brokers charge for their services. With thousands of dollars at stake, it isn't surprising that many people find FSBO tempting, but they usually quote other non-financial reasons for going this route:

- **Control.** Some people hate being at the beck and call of agents and their client viewings and value being able to schedule viewings for times that suit them—and not having to live in "show home" conditions on permanent standby.
- **Local Expertise.** FSBO enthusiasts often feel they are the best people to sell their home because they are the people who know the most about it—and the surrounding area.
- **Flexibility.** You can try the FSBO route for just a few weeks if you want to "test the waters" without being tied into a six-month real estate listing contract.

Although there are a growing number of Internet sites that are designed to support FSBO promotion, these have nothing like the penetration of the MLS system. Instead, they tend to attract the equally independent minded buyer who is not using a buyer's agent with access to the MLS database.

Figures from the National Association of Realtors suggest that these limitations are reflected in the experiences of FSBO sellers.

It appears from their statistics that over 80% of people who try FSBO end up listing with a real estate agent within six to eight weeks—and say they wouldn't try FSBO again.

While I can certainly applaud the independent spirit that drives FSBO, I cannot recommend it for anyone who is likely to be reading this book. If so many native Floridians consistently find that FSBO doesn't work for them, I fear there is little hope for anyone without a very detailed knowledge of the Florida real estate system.

If for some reason you find yourself in a situation where you feel FSBO is the best or only option available to you, the best advice I can give is to concentrate on these elements:

- **Promotion**. The agent-driven MLS system is the standard system for anyone to find property in Florida.
- With that avenue closed off to you, you will have to work 10 times as hard to get a decent amount of exposure for your property.
- **Price**. FSBO sellers consistently overprice their properties because they do not fully understand the market—or the market value of their property.
- This is especially a problem because most of the buyers that are attracted to FSBO properties are those that are looking for a cut-price bargain.
- Agent listing fees can quickly be justified if you get access to qualified, funded buyers who are willing to pay the market price. At least get an independent valuation done to establish a fair price to ask.
- **Research**. Many FSBO sellers ignore the details that every buyer wants to know.
- Facts and figures about sizes, dates and amenities are critical, so you should either buy a DIY pro-forma to gather all this information or try and get your hands on a listing form from a real estate agent.
- **Due Diligence**. There is a lot of work done in the back offices of real estate companies and the other professionals involved in non-FSBO sales that no-one ever sees. Public

records are checked, insurance details are gathered, title information is extracted and checked, mortgage details are confirmed and recorded, and much more.
- Best of all, these people assume a professional liability for the work they do—indemnifying you from problems that arise if they make a mistake. With FSBO, you have to do all that work yourself—and the penalties for getting it wrong could be very serious indeed.

SELLER'S AGENTS

If you have read this book sequentially, you will appreciate the importance of the buyer's agent in helping you find the right property and negotiate the Florida real estate system.

Well, exactly the same is true when selling—and your best ally in the sales process will be a seller's agent with the same kind of experience.

If you have already gone through that process, hopefully you had a good experience with your agent working with you as a buyer. More than 80% of people who use a REALTOR® (that's a member of the National Association of Realtors—the only people who can put REALTOR® on their business cards) say they would use them again, so this is obviously the best place to start your search for an agent to work with.

A few agents may heavily specialise in either buying or selling, but in most cases they do both, so you can save a lot of time getting to know a new agent and their back office systems by getting back in touch with your previous agent. All of my previous comments about buyer's agents—how they work, how to find one, fiduciary responsibilities, etc—are all relevant here too, so you may want to review that chapter before going on.

The Listing Contract

Once you have found a real estate professional you want to use as your agent, you will sign a listing contract with them. Also referred to as a listing agreement, this authorises them to act on your behalf in the sale of your property. Listing contracts vary greatly, but there are some characteristics that are common to all.

Any valid listing contract must be in writing and should include:

- **Employment.** The listing contract is a personal services contract between you and the broker. It contains all of the terms and conditions that relate to you employing the broker and authorising them to represent you in marketing and selling your property.
- **Compensation.** For any contract to be valid, there has to be "compensation"—which basically means, "if I do this, you will do that". The listing contract will specify the amount and timing of payment to your broker. Typically, payment is a percentage of the sales price, payable at closing.
- It is important to note that your obligation to pay your broker may not absolutely depend on a finalised sales transaction. If the broker finds a genuine buyer who is willing to pay your asking price and agrees to the terms you have offered, but you for some reason you decide not to sell to them, the broker has done his job and is entitled to be paid under the terms of the listing contract.
- **Title.** All listing contracts will ask who has title to the property. Property can't be sold unless everyone who holds title interest in the property is part of the sale.
- **Termination Date.** The most common duration of a listing contract is 180 days, but you shouldn't sign any listing contract that doesn't have a specific termination date—including contracts that include terms such as "until sold". The listing contract is a legally binding document and you don't want to get locked into one with no clearly defined termination date.
- If the contract expires before your home sells and you still want to keep using the same broker, you can simply sign a new contract.

This is a simplified view of a listing contract and there will typically be more clauses within it. As with any legal document, you should read the listing contract very carefully, be sure you understand exactly what you are agreeing to and if necessary take legal advice before signing.

Time To Promote

The listing contract is the permission your agent needs to start marketing your home by listing it on the MLS database and any other promotional methods they have at their disposal; leaflets and brochures, websites, print advertising, etc.

For your part, you have to be prepared for viewings at any time. Especially if you are not currently living in the property, agents will usually have access to show prospective buyers around at any time.

Setting The Price

Your agent will initially do a Comparative Market Analysis (CMA) that will show the listing price of similar houses in the area as well as the prices at which the houses actually sold.

Remember that all agents have access to the central MLS, so they can also look at how many similar properties are currently on the market and how many have been recently offered but were never sold.

The agent combines these factors with the influence of other market conditions that may be local (is it a buyer's or seller's market in this region) and national (interest rates for example) *plus* your needs with regard to speed of sale and price, to arrive at a recommendation of the price at which your property should be listed.

SELL, SELL, SELL

Your agent will highlight any key problems they think are serious enough to affect your chance of a sale—or of getting the price you want—before promoting the property fully.

If all the major issues have been addressed but there is no real activity after the property has been on the market for a few months, it's time to re-evaluate. The reason for the lack of interest is almost certainly contained below.

Check The Price

By far the most common reason for a home not selling is that the asking price has been set too high. The reasons for setting your price too high to begin with are many, ranging from over enthusiastic listing agents to unrealistic seller expectations.

No matter what the reason, an overpriced property is a problem on several levels. Even if you do get an offer for your asking price, the deal may fall apart before closing because the buyer may have problems getting finance—especially if the property doesn't appraise for anything close to your asking price.

Look at other homes for sale that are as close as possible to yours in terms of size, features and location. Look not only at asking prices—but the price they have recently sold for. If they are less than you are asking, you may be priced too high. It will hurt to drop your price, but the only valuation that matters is the price the market is willing to pay.

Check The Condition

Your home has to compete against other similar homes for sale, as well as competing against shiny brand new homes and all the marketing clout that developers can throw at their latest project.

The more you can do to make your home look appealing to a buyer, the better your chances for a quick sale. Look at your home with a critical buyer's eye and see what they see. After the low-cost ideas in the section that follows, the next best value-for-money improvements are paint and flooring.

Make sure that all your paint is in great condition, inside and out. Repainting needn't cost too much, and will usually make the biggest impact on buyers. Then make sure all of the flooring looks good too. You may want to consider putting in new carpet, rugs or runners. Again, it doesn't have to be expensive but it does make a positive impact on buyers.

Location, location, location

It's the oldest cliché in the world—and I've said it so much that it should probably be the sub-title for this book.

But it's true.

If you're in a bad location, a good real estate agent may be able to help minimise some of the impact by suggesting improvements to the house. But the only really reliable way to overcome a bad location problem is with a lower price. Simply put, an identical home in a bad location won't sell for as much as the same home in a better location.

Promotion

Is your agent living up to their promises about how they would promote your property?

The best agents have an aggressive marketing plan that typically includes online marketing, local newspapers, magazines and real estate publications, making sure other local agents know about the property—and even running radio and TV ads.

If all your agent has done is put a sign in your front yard and add your home to the local MLS, then that agent isn't coming close to doing all that can be done to effectively market your home.

Market Problems

Blaming the market is often just an excuse for bad pricing, promotion or some other problem, but sometimes it's true.

If there are too many comparable homes for sale and not enough active buyers, it is going to be hard to get a quick sale and a great price. The best way to beat a slow market is to simply wait it out, but that's not always an option for many sellers. The only other alternative is either to drop the selling price or offer other concessions—like paying some fixed costs—to attract buyers who might be watching every last penny.

Open All Hours

Can everyone who wants to see your house see it at the time that suits them?

If an agent is arranging a series of viewings for a client, it's only natural that they will take the path of least resistance and prioritise those properties with easiest access. Many homes on the market have "lock boxes" on them.

The lock box is a device that holds a key to the home, that only qualified local agents can access. Homes that are listed as being "lock box, no appointment needed" will get shown more often than homes listed as "agent has key, call for appointment". If at all possible, you should let your agent put a lock box on your home for easier showing.

Easy Improvements

There are however a few things you can do at little or no cost to present the house in its best light and make a positive impression on people who come to view it.

Let in the light:
- Prune bushes and trees outside windows
- Keep curtains light and well pulled back during the day
- Use soft light bulbs to create a warm glow in the evening

Use fragrance:
- Place cut flowers in a welcoming position close to the entrance
- Put out potpourri
- Burn scented candles

Buy new:
- Doormat
- Mailbox
- House number/nameplate

Outside impressions:
- Freshen any gravel or stone chippings on driveways
- Edge the grass around paths and trees
- Use external lighting if you have it
- Clean your gutters

Reduce clutter:
- Downsize your possessions and lighten the load
- Keep your garden tools out of sight
- Keep the kids' toys out of sight

TAX FOR SELLERS

There are a number of tax issues to consider when selling your property, especially if—as you hope—the property has increased in value during your ownership.

If you think you will be exposed to a tax liability, it is worth getting advice from a tax specialist as early as possible as there may well be steps you can take to minimise or eradicate the size of the tax bill.

Capital Gains

Capital gains tax liability on sale of a property in Florida should be relatively rare—especially for couples jointly owning a property. Subject to certain conditions, you would have to generate a *profit* of more than $500,000 on a property in joint-ownership before you would have a capital gains tax liability, and there are investment and time-related clauses that may exempt you from even that.

Foreign Investors Real Property Tax Act

FIRPTA is a particularly nasty piece of legislation for foreign property owners. Once you have invested your money in US property, the American government is very worried you will sell the property and skip the country with the money.

Under FIRPTA, the agent handling the sale of your property is required to withhold 10% of the gross price you sell for—even if you have not made a profit. It *is* possible to get an advance clearance from the IRS, but you should start the process several months before you plan to sell.

There is an exception to this, which many closing agents are not aware of. If the property is sold for less that $300,000 and the buyer (or a member of their family) is going to use it as a personal residence, no withholding tax should be deducted.

Inheritance tax

In Florida, this is known as "Estate Tax" and again, the allowances are generous. You (or your heirs) don't have to file inheritance-related income where your total assets are (currently) less than $1,500,000—and there are of course ways a good accountant can help you minimise that liability.

APPENDIX A
Glossary

An explanation of terms used in this book plus others you will come across in the Florida property world. Where possible, the equivalent UK term is given—or if the UK equivalent is the same or non-existent.

USA Term	UK Term
Explanation of term	

Agreement of Sale or Real Estate Contract	Counterpart Contracts
A written document in which a purchaser agrees to buy property, which the vendor agrees to sell, under certain agreed conditions. Also known as a 'Sales Contract'.	
Alimony	**Child Support payments**
Regular and continuing payments paid to an ex-spouse/partner	

Amortization	Capital Repayment
The process of gradually paying off the principal of the loan. As each payment toward principal is made, the mortgage amount is reduced or amortized by that amount. This is different to an interest-only mortgage payment where the principal balance is not reduced over the term.	
Amortized Loan	**Capital Repayment Loan**
A loan that is completely paid off, interest and principal, by a series of regular payments that are equal or nearly equal.	
Application	**Same Term**
A form commonly referred to as a 1003 form, used to apply for a mortgage and to provide information regarding a prospective mortgagor and the proposed security.	
Application Fee	
see 'Origination Fee'	
Appraisal	**Valuation**

An estimate of the market value of a piece of real estate made by a competent professional (the appraiser) who knows local property market and prices.	
Approval	**Agreement in Principle**
An assessment made of an applicant's ability to pay for a home and confirmation of the amount the applicant may borrow.	
Assessed Value	**Council Tax**
The value of a property for tax purposes set by a tax assessor according to a formula.	
Assessments	**No Equivalent**
Special and local taxes imposed upon property which benefits from an improvement that has been made in the area.	
Auto Pay or ACH Payment	**Direct Debit**
A method to set up a regular payment to be automatically paid from a bank account.	

Binder	**No Equivalent**
An agreement to consider the purchase of real estate. The agreement is secured and backed by a cash deposit as evidence of good faith on the part of the purchaser.	
Broker	**Agent**
A person or firm who acts on behalf of another.	
Building Insurance	
see 'Hazard Insurance'	
Cash Reserves	**Surplus**
Refers to amount of cash held by a borrower after the purchase is complete (i.e. after down payment, closing costs, etc.)	
Cash-Out Refinance	**Equity Release**

A refinance transaction in which the amount of money received from the new loan exceeds the total of the money needed to repay the existing first mortgage, closing costs and the amount required to redeem other mortgages against the property.

In short, a refinance transaction in which the borrower receives additional cash that can be used for any acceptable purpose.

Certificate of Title	Title Deeds

A written document stating that the title to a piece of property is legally vested in the present owner.

Clear Title	Unencumbered

Title not burdened by mortgages, charges (liens) or legal questions.

Closing	Completion

In property transactions, the delivery of a deed, the payment of the purchase price, the signing of notes, and the paying of closing costs, which completes the transaction.

Closing Costs	Disbursements

The various expenses involved in closing a property transaction that are in addition to the purchase price. Closing costs can include title insurance, appraisal fee, and credit report.

Closing Statement	Settlement Statement

Can be known as the 'HUD-1'. The final statement of costs to be paid to close a loan or to purchase a property.

Collateral	Security

Any property given as security for repayment of a debt.

Combined Loan-to-Value (CLTV)	Equity

The relationship between the money owed on all the mortgages on a property (first and second etc) and the property's appraised value (or sales price, if it is lower).

Commission or Broker Fee	Offer of Advance

A broker's fee for negotiating a real estate or loan transaction, often expressed as a percentage of the purchase price or the loan amount.	
Commitment Letter	
A formal offer which states the terms under which it has been agreed to lend money. Also known as a 'loan commitment'. This letter will indicate the conditions that must be satisfied before release of funds.	
Condominium	**Flat**
A structure of two or more housing units. Only interior area of a particular unit is individually owned. All the owners of the individual units jointly own the remainder of the property (land, building and other amenities).	
Contingency	**Pre-Contractual Stipulation**
A clause or condition within a contract stating what the buyer or seller must satisfy before the purchase can be completed.	
Co-operative	**No Equivalent**

A residential development owned by a co-operative corporation. Residents own shares in the co-operative, which in turn gives them the right to live in the development.	
Counterpart Contracts	
see 'Agreement of Sale'.	
Council Tax	
see 'Assessed Value'	
Deposit	
see 'Down Payment'	
Down Payment	**Deposit**
The agreed percentage of the purchase price a buyer pays, in cash, at the time the property transaction closes ('completes').	
Dwelling Coverage	**'All Inclusive' coverage**

Insurance coverage protects your property and any structures attached to it, like the garage or screened porch. Any materials on your property that are being used to extend or repair the fabric of the building, such as timber or bricks being used for an improvement, would also be covered.

Earthquake Insurance	**No Equivalent**

Insurance that compensates for damage to a property resulting from earthquakes. The extent of coverage is limited by the terms of the policy.

Escrow Disbursements	**No Equivalent**

Use of escrow funds to pay real estate taxes, hazard insurance, mortgage insurance, and other property expenses as they become due.

Escrow Fee	**No Equivalent**

Fee charged by the escrow company for handling escrow activities including paying off mortgages and clearing title and other debts.

Estate Agent	
see 'Realtor'	
Fair Market Value	**Open Market Value**
A figure that is the highest amount a purchaser would agree to pay for a property and the lowest amount the vendor would be prepared to sell at.	
Finance Charge	**Total as Charge for Credit**
Charges levied that include all of the interest due over the life of a loan, in addition to certain other charges related to a loan.	
Flood Insurance	**Same Term**
A form of insurance designed to reimburse property owners from loss due to the defined peril of flood. It is required for properties located in federally designated flood areas.	
Foreclosure	**Repossession**

Legal process by which a borrower in default under the terms of a mortgage ceases to have an interest in the mortgaged property. This usually involves a forced sale of the property at public auction with the proceeds of the sale being used to reduce or clear the mortgage debt.	
Good Faith Estimate	**No Equivalent**
A disclosure that must be given to all mortgage loan applicants within three business days of an application. It is an estimate of all costs likely to be incurred at closing.	
Guarantor	
see 'Signer'	
HUD	**No Equivalent**
The US Department of Housing and Urban Development.	
Hazard Insurance	**Building Insurance**

Insurance protecting against loss to property caused by fire, some natural causes, vandalism, etc., depending upon the terms of the policy.	
Homeowners Insurance Declaration	**Insurance Schedule**
A document accompanying a homeowners insurance policy whose purpose is to verify that the property quoted is insured.	
Income Property	**Rental Property**
Properties owned with intention of producing an income. Also referred to as 'non-owner occupied property' or 'rental property.'	
Installment	**Mortgage Payment**
The regular monthly payment that a borrower agrees to pay.	
Loan Processing	**Underwriting**

Steps taken from the time a loan application is received to the time the application is approved or declined. This process includes receiving the application, credit searches (investigation) and the overall underwriting assessment of the application.	
Loan Terms	**Mortgage Conditions**
Necessary conditions of a loan which specify the amount borrowed, interest rate, maturity, method of repayment, etc.	
Loan to Value (LTV)	**No Equivalent**
The percentage size of the loan in relation to the value of the property.	
Low-Documentation	**Self Declaration**
Below a stated LTV, only requires the applicant to state the source and the affordability of the mortgage applied for without providing supporting documentation, pay slips or trading accounts.	
Market Value	**Open Market Value**

Also known as 'Fair Market Value.' The professionally considered estimated value of the property that a seller could expect to receive under normal conditions.

| Maisonette | |

see 'Multi-Family'

| Maturity | Loan Term |

The term of a loan, or the number or years for which the loan funds are advanced.

| Mortgage Payment | |

see 'Installment'

| Multi-Family | Flat/Maisonette |

A building with more than four residential units.

| Origination Date | Completion Date |

The date on which the loan is applied for.

| Origination Fee | Application Fee |

A fee imposed to cover the administrative costs of setting up a mortgage. This may include the preparation of documents and certain processing expenses in connection with completing a mortgage account.	
Owner Occupant	**Owner-Occupier**
A borrower who intends to permanently reside in the property used as security for the loan.	
Payoff	**Redemption**
Complete repayment/settlement of the principal balance along with interest and any other amounts due. The payoff of an account occurs either over the full term of the mortgage through monthly repayments or through early redemption.	
Planned Unit Developments (PUD)	**No Equivalent**
A subdivision of five or more individually owned lots with one or more other parcels owned in common or with reciprocal rights in one or more other parcels.	
Pre-Approval	**Decision in**

	Principle
A process, in which you will be offered an opinion as to what products, if any, are available to the applicant. The pre-approval is not binding and not necessarily accurate because we will not have yet verified the application details.	
Preliminary Title Report	**No Equivalent**
A report made by a title company stating whether there are any other claims to ownership of a property. A necessary step before a mortgage loan can be approved.	
Prepaids	**Pre-payments**
Those purchase expenses that are paid in advance of their due date and will usually be pro-rated upon sale, such as taxes, insurance, rent, etc.	
Pre-payment Clause	**Redemption Penalty Clause**

A clause that confirms the amount of the principal balance of an account the borrower may pay earlier that expected with or without penalty. The terms vary according to the product selected.

Pre-payment Penalty	**Redemption Penalty**
A charge a borrower pays to redeem or part redeem a loan before it is due.	

Promissory Note	
Your Loan Agreement with the Lender detailing all the rights, obligations and conditions of the Loan.	

Realtor	**Estate Agent/Property Developer**
A real estate broker or an associate holding active membership in a real estate board affiliated with the National Association of Realtors.	

Refinancing	**Remortgaging**

Taking out a new loan to pay off an existing mortgage. This is usually done to obtain a lower interest rate or to borrow further funds against the equity in a property that may have built up since the original purchase.

RESPA Real Estate Settlement Procedures Act Sales Contract	**Purchase Contract**

A written agreement between the vendor and purchaser stating the conditions that need satisfying for the sale to complete. Also known as an 'Agreement of Sale.'

Signer	**Guarantor**

A person who signs a promissory note along with the borrower. A co-maker's signature guarantees that the loan will be repaid, because the borrower and the co-maker are jointly and severally liable for the total debt owed.

Title Insurance	**Same Term**

The insurance that protects your mortgage company, along with the homeowner if an owner's policy is purchased, against losses resulting from problems with the title of a property, or unknown liens (charges) or other inconsistencies relating to the title of the property.	
Title Report	**No Equivalent**
A report that discloses whether there are any competing claims, liens (charges) or other ownership issues relating to the security address. This is done before title insurance is issued. Also known as a 'Preliminary Title Report'.	
Truth-in-Lending Act (TILA)	
A law applicable in the United States requiring disclosure of credit terms of the finance transaction using a recognized format. This is intended to help borrowers compare the lending costs, terms and conditions of different lenders. Also known as 'Regulation Z.'	

BUYING & SELLING PROPERTY IN FLORIDA
A UK RESIDENTS GUIDE

The author has assembled an experienced team of experts who are able to help you with all aspects of Florida property purchase, sale, management and other issues. Please visit the following websites for information or email the author directly at: sparnell@lynxbanc.com

www.LynxBanc.co.uk
www.AskSteveParnell.co.uk